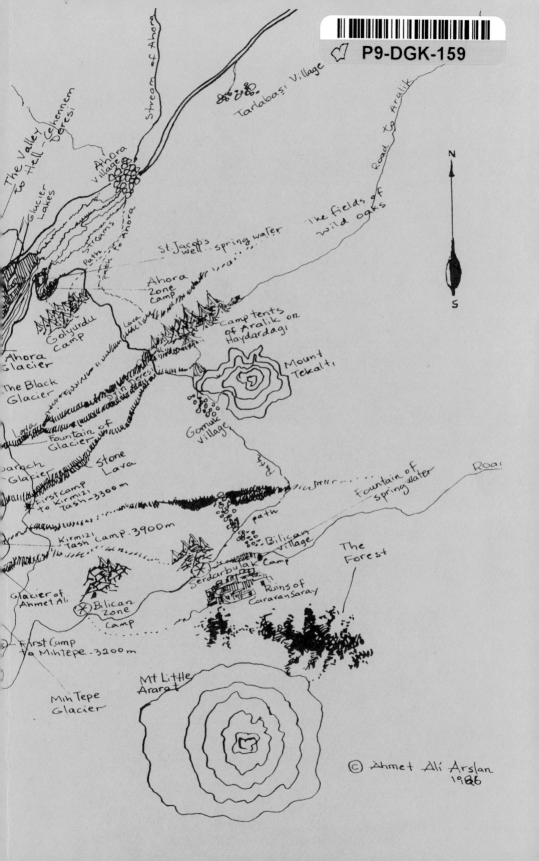

The Valley to Hell – Cehennem Deresi

Stream of Ahora

Tartabaşı Village

Road to Aralık

Glacier Lakes

Ahora Village

N

Streams to Ahora

Path

Path to Ahora

St Jacob's well – spring water

The fields of wild oaks

S

Ahora Zone Camp

Golyurdu Camp

Lava

Camp tents of Aralık on Haydardağı

Ahora Glacier

Jin Deresi

Mount Tekalti

The Black Glacier

Lava

Fountain of Glacier

Gomuk Village

Darach Glacier

Stone Lava

First Camp to Kirmizi Tash – 3300 m

Kirmizi Tash Camp – 3900 m

Fountain of spring water

Road

path

Bilican Village

Serdarbulak Camp

The Forest

Glacier of Ahmet Ali

Bilican Zone Camp

Ruins of Caravansaray

First Camp to Mihtepe – 3200 m

Mt Little Ararat

Mih Tepe Glacier

© Ahmet Ali Arslan 1986

THE LOST SHIP
of
NOAH

Other Books by Charles Berlitz

Atlantis: The Eighth Continent
Native Tongues
Doomsday 1999 A.D.
The Philadelphia Experiment (with Wm. Moore)
Without a Trace
The Bermuda Triangle
Mysteries From Forgotten Worlds
The Mystery of Atlantis
Dive (revision)

THE LOST SHIP
of
NOAH

In Search of the Ark at Ararat

CHARLES BERLITZ

with appreciation to
Ahmet Ali Arslan
for his photographs, drawings,
maps, and information pertinent
to his numerous ascents of
Mount Ararat

G. P. Putnam's Sons
New York

G. P. Putnam's Sons
Publishers Since 1838
200 Madison Avenue
New York, NY 10016

Typeset by Fisher Composition, Inc.

Library of Congress Cataloging-in-Publication Data

Berlitz, Charles Frambach, date.
The lost ship of Noah.

Bibliography: p.
Includes index.
1. Noah's ark. 2. Ararat, Mount (Turkey)
I. Title.
DS51.A66B47   1987   222'.11093   86-25141
ISBN 0-399-13182-5

Printed in the United States of America
1 2 3 4 5 6 7 8 9 10

Contents

THE LOST SHIP
of
NOAH

1

The Ship
on the Mountain

High above the Anatolian plateau in Eastern Turkey, only several miles from the borders of Iran and Russia, a sudden mountain rises from the plains. It is not among the world's highest (17,011 feet), but its name has long been most famous among mountains. Its name for thousands of years has been a message to the majority of the world's peoples—the name that promises, teaches, commands, and sometimes threatens. That name is Ararat.

Ararat, site of the reputed landing of Noah's Ark on its summit after the Great Flood, has been a part of Christian belief for almost 2000 years, of Judaic belief even longer, of Babylonian belief before that, and Sumerian before it was a legend in Babylon, with another name *(Ut-Napishtim)* for Noah. Moslem tradition has immortalized Noah *(Nūh* in Arabic) and the great ship, although it is less certain of the location of the mountain where it landed, referring to it as *Al Judi* ("the heights") sometimes applied to Ararat or to two other mountains in the Middle East. The Book of Genesis gives an approximate location, stating that "the Ark came to rest in

the mountains of Ararat." This latter name is a deriva-
tion of *Urartu,* a name for ancient Armenia. But popular belief among the nations in the Ararat area, as well
as among the majority of the spiritual descendants of
the "peoples of the book" which includes Christians,
Jews, and Moslems is that the landing place of the Ark
was Mount Ararat, perhaps because it is the highest,
most formidable, and most difficult to climb, among the
"Mountains of Armenia."

Over the centuries Mount Ararat, observed by
passing travelers on horseback, mules, and camel caravans to and from inner Asia have reported that they
had observed a great ship near the top of the mountain
or had spoken with local people who said they had not
only seen it but had visited it. These natives had even
taken bits of pitch from the covering of the Ark from
which they made amulets for protection against sickness, disaster, against being poisoned, or for success in
love.

In modern times, since the early 1800s, Ararat has
been climbed by teams of mountaineers equipped with
peak-scaling equipment, quadrants, height indicators,
and cameras. These expeditions have not yet found any
definite wreck of a huge ship on the mountain, other
than shiplike shadows under the glaciers or beams of
worked wood in or under the ice near the summit. The
belief has grown that the Ark has slipped down the
mountain and has fallen or descended into a giant crevasse, deeply frozen into one of the several glaciers
which flow down Ararat.

The presence of an ancient ship on the summit of
Ararat or of any high mountain would seem to be solely
a survival of an ancient legend combined with a religious and moral message for succeeding generations.
Looking at the mountain from the plains or foothills

and reflecting on the fascinating story of Noah and the Ark it is easy to see, or imagine that one sees, the shape of a ship in the serrated formations of the ridges, a long oval shape in the gorges, or an unexplained black rectangular spot along the glaciers. But the many persons who have reported seeing a ship on Ararat, especially during the last 200 years, were not looking at it from afar but sometimes from high up on the mountain or, according to their reports, in the immediate proximity of part of a huge ship, the greater portion of which extended back into the glacial ice.

The paradox of how a ship could survive for thousands of years on top of a mountain is not insoluble. First we must accept the theory of a great flood—of tidal waves that washed over the plains, valleys, and mountains of the earth, bearing with them the wreckage of a destroyed civilization. The Ark of Ararat would be one survivor of such a flood, as may have been the case with other ships of rescue referred to in all ancient and prehistoric cultures in mankind's oldest common legend. For the story of the Flood is worldwide as is the story of the survival by ship of a favored man and woman, usually with other family members or followers together with animals and plants for the renewal of life in a devastated world. Only the name of Noah and the kinds of animals he took with him varies in the many parts of the planet where the legend has been preserved. The local stories so resemble each other that when the Spanish first came to the New World they found the civilized Indian nations as well as the forest tribes already familiar with the epic of the Flood. Some of the *conquistadores* considered this familiarity with Christian religious tradition to be simply a trick of the Devil to cause confusion among true believers.

That an event of such magnitude as a world flood

should be remembered by surviving generations is understandable. But the legend of a great wooden ship
surviving for thousands of years, outlasting great cities
and entire civilizations, is considerably less credible. As
wood, iron, copper, brick, steel, and all building mate-
rials except huge stones vanish with time, how could a
wooden ship maintain its recognizable shape on a
mountaintop? To this question there is an answer: it
would if it were frozen. The summit of Ararat, the
glacier between the two peaks, and the inner folds of the
deep glaciers slowly moving down its flanks are cold
enough for preserving a craft made of heavy timbers
and caulked, in the words of Genesis, ". . . within and
without with pitch." The occasional sightings by climbers and airborne pilots of a shiplike object on Ararat
have invariably indicated a section of a great barge with
the main part retreating into and under the ice, or a
shadow *under* the ice which appears to follow the lines of
a ship with the approximate dimensions of the Ark as
detailed in Genesis: "The length of the Ark shall be
three hundred cubits, the breadth of it fifty cubits, and
the height of it thirty cubits."

One might suggest that both of these above pos-
sibilities are essentially the same if one considers climatic
variations. Every twenty years or so an especially hot
spell affects the Ararat region, and it is usually at these
times, especially during the normally hot months of August and early September, that sightings of a ship have
been reported. While the object remains under the ice it
stays impervious to decay, just as extinct animals like the
mammoths of Siberia and the saber-tooth tigers and
other Pleistocene mammals found in Alaska and Northern Canada which have been dug out of the ice complete with their fur and skin and with undigested food
from a pre-glacial age still in their stomachs.

Since snow and ice rarely recede from certain areas of Mount Ararat, explorers may have climbed over vestiges of a great ship without realizing it. If the ship is still on the mountain deep under the snow and ice, prolonged and specialized investigation would be needed, especially difficult to accomplish on a mountain so dangerous to climb that for centuries local superstition has held it to be supernaturally protected from climbers searching for the Ark. This assumed protection covers a multitude of dangers: avalanches, sudden rock slides, violent electric storms, and high winds near the summit. Fast-forming fogs disorient climbers and often lead them to snow-covered or lightly frozen areas over deep crevasses which subsequently become their tombs. There are also a number of living dangers: poisonous snakes near the bottom of the mountain and, continuing upward, wolf packs and equally dangerous wild dogs, bears that pre-empt caves where a climber might seek shelter and, from time to time, and quite recently, Kurdish insurgents. All of this might have suggested to would-be explorers of the mountain that the summit had been put "off limits" by even higher forces than the ever watchful local gendarmerie.

But the searchers have not interrupted their efforts. The search for the ship on Ararat continues, seemingly intensifying every year during the months of late summer when much of the ice has melted. For the prize—the discovery of the major section of the Ark—so often reported by climbers on the mountain or observers from the air, is incalculable. It could modify our concept of ancient history, reassess the geological history of the world, and reaffirm the traditional religious beliefs of a great section of the world's peoples. In this the Ark becomes timeless, affecting the future as well as the past.

2

Ancient References— Contemporary Confirmations

Many of the historic references to sightings of a ship on Mount Ararat as seen from the ground have been made by observers visiting cities with a view of the mountain. Other sightings have been recorded by travelers who moved slowly across the Anatolian Plain in caravans as they journeyed to and from Persia, Armenia, and the Tartar lands to the north, now part of the USSR. In ancient and medieval times, when faith was stronger and men were less skeptical, the presence of Noah's Ark on Ararat was generally accepted as an actuality. Therefore, as travelers passed by the mountain their guides would customarily point out places on the slopes or the summit where Noah's Ark might still be seen. And, in the clear light of early morning, before the clouds cover the summit, or in the dusk, when the clouds have gone

15

and the black shapes of the crests appear against the rose colored or violet sky of early evening, it becomes easy for a believer, or even an imaginative nonbeliever, to discern the outline of a great ship on the heights.

Although there exist a great number of references to the Ark in ancient or medieval history, some of them refer to particulars which later became familiar to modern searchers for the Ark. Berossus, a Babylonian historian writing in 275 B.C., referred to "the ship that grounded in Armenia" and mentioned the custom of local residents who obtained "pitch from the ship by scraping it off and using it for amulets." This same curious piece of information intrigued the Jewish historian Flavius Josephus, writing in the first century during the Roman occupation of Judea. In retelling the story of Noah and the Flood, Josephus wrote, "a portion of the vessel still survives in Armenia . . . persons carry off pieces of the bitumen which they use as talismans. . . ." A tradition of the late Middle Ages recommended that the pitch be ground into powder and dissolved into a beverage to be then drunk to preserve he who drank it from poison.

> Comment: *References to pitch and bitumen by these and other ancient writers are of interest not only because they are in agreement with Genesis but also because they indicate access to the huge ship in the intervening centuries and also offer an explanation as to why some worked beams and timbers found high on the mountain under the ice may have been well preserved.*

Flavius Josephus included an interesting note in his *History of the Jews*: "The Armenians called this place "The Place of Descent" for the Ark being saved in that place its remains are shown there by the inhabitants to this day."

Nicolaus of Damascus, who wrote universal history in the first century A.D., refers to Mount Ararat as *Baris:* ". . . there is in Armenia a great mountain called Baris, where many refugees found safety at the time of the Flood, and one man, transported on an Ark, grounded on the summit, and relics of the timbers were long preserved."

> *Baris was another name for the present Mount Ararat which, in Armenia, is referred to as Massis, "The Mother of the World." Nicolaus exhibits a somewhat scholarly reticence to jumping to conclusions when he reflectively adds ". . . this might be the same man of which Moses, the Jewish legislator, wrote. . . ."*

One of the most famous travelers of history passed by Ararat in the last part of the fifteenth century. This was Marco Polo on his way to the court of the great Khan in Cathay. In his book *Travels of Marco Polo* he made an intriguing reference to the Ark: ". . . You must know that it is in this country of Armenia that the Ark of Noah exists on the top of a certain great mountain on the summit of which snow is so constant that no one can ascend; for the snow never melts and it is constantly added to by new falls. Below, however, the snow does melt and runs down, producing such rich and abundant herbage that in summer cattle are sent to pasture from a long roundabout way and it never fails them."

> *Marco Polo's description still fits Mount Ararat, except for the statement that no one can ascend it. The*

important point that the snow and ice melts on the bottom and runs under the glaciers is especially noteworthy since it has been in certain crevasses under the glaciers that modern investigators have found ancient handworked beams and timbers.

A German visitor to the area in the early seventeenth century, Adam Oelschläger (in Latin, Olearius), observes, in his *Voyages and Travels of the Ambassadors*: "The Armenians and the Persians themselves are of the opinion that there are still, on the said mountain, some remainders of the Ark, but that time has so hardened them that they seem to be absolutely petrified."

Olearius' mention of the petrification of timbers fits in with actual timbers brought back from the treeless glacial slopes of the mountain, which now can be seen in the monastery of Echmiadzin and which also resemble pieces of the alleged Ark brought back in modern times by the French explorer-mountaineer Fernand Navarra and further remains discovered by other explorers.

Sir John Mandeville saw the mountain in 1356 and, dazzled by its sheer height, most apparent in the early morning before the clouds hide the summit, was one of the first observers to attempt an estimate of its height. He describes: "A mountain called Ararat . . . where Noah's ship rested and still is upon that mountain and men see it afar in clear weather. That mountain is full seven miles high. . . ."

As Ararat is actually 17,011 feet high this type of overenthusiasm tends to minimize Sir John's other observations on Mount Ararat. It is understandable,

*however, when one takes into account Ararat's sudden
and awe inspiring appearance when the clouds lift. Dr.
John Montgomery, in* The Quest for Noah's Ark, *suggests that Mandeville may have been calculating the
distance from the foothills to the top of the peak.*

The many writers of antiquity and the Middle Ages
who have described Ararat apparently did not feel
called upon to attempt to climb up its sides, facing its
glaciers, precipices, rock slides and avalanches to find
out firsthand whether or not the Ark was still there. In
their day it was not really necessary. Religious faith before the era of doubt which initiated the modern age
needed no reaffirmation and, in addition, there was always the threat of divine interdiction against profaning
the holy vessel. The Christian population of Europe and
the Middle East, from the days of the Byzantine Empire, firmly believed that the Ark was on Mount Ararat
and the later teachings of Islam reinforced the belief in
the Flood, the Ark, and Nūh (Noah) and that the Ark
would only be revealed by God on the Day of Judgment.

A Franciscan friar, Odoric, who was later to report
back to the papal court at Avignon, saw the mountain in
1316 and related: ". . . the folk in the country told us
that no one could ever ascend the mountain for this . . .
hath seemed not to be the pleasure of the Most
High. . . ." Odoric himself, alone among ancient or medieval commentators, was seemingly unimpressed by
the sheer height of the threatening mountain. More
than four hundred years before the first recorded ascent, he wrote: ". . . I would fain have ascended it if my
companions would have waited for me. . . ."

Belief in the Ark was then and often is now an
article of faith, some Byzantine churchmen referring to

the Ark as a standing proof of the Church's teachings. John Chrysostom, a fourth-century patriach of Constantinople, asked questions to which he thought the answers were amply evident: "Let us therefore ask they who do not believe: Have you heard of the Flood—of that universal destruction? That was not just a threat, was it? Did it not really come to pass—was not this mighty work carried out? And are not the remains of the Ark preserved there to this very day for our admonition?"

In like fashion Bishop Epiphanius of Salamis asked: "Do you seriously suppose that we are unable to prove our point, when even to this day the remains of Noah's Ark are shown in the country of the Kurds?"

This fourth-century reference to the Kurds suggests that they were already established around the mountain along with the Armenians at a very early date. The Armenians are gone, mainly concentrated in the Armenian SSR of the USSR and in communities within the USA. The Kurds still live in the Mount Ararat area and from time to time engage in raids and warfare against local governments in Kurdish-populated areas in the Middle East.

The legend of God's prohibition against man's ascending Mount Ararat has lasted until fairly modern times. Dr. Friedrich Parrot, a German professor of natural philosophy from Dorpat University, Estonia, then part of Imperial Russia, made the first "official" climb to the summit in 1829, giving his name to the Parrot Glacier, which flows northwest down the mountain. Parrot observed of his Russian and Armenian climbing companions: "They are all firmly persuaded that the

Ark remains to this day on the top of Mount Ararat, and that in order to ensure its preservation no human being is allowed to approach it." Previous to his climb Parrot spent some time at St. Jacob's monastery at Ahora on the northwest side of the mountain and was shown by the abbot some wood reportedly from the Ark which had been made into an ikon. However, the monastery, monks, and village of Ahora disappeared in 1840 during Mount Ararat's last volcanic eruption, which buried the monastery and village and left a precipitous gorge where the buildings had been.

Dr. Hermann Abich, another German professor (mineralogy), also from the University of Dorpat, climbed Ararat in 1845. Abich's name has been immortalized in the two Abich glaciers, one of which noisily empties its waters into the Ahora Gorge on the northeast side of the mountain that looks toward Russia. Although Abich was not specifically looking for the Ark, one of his reasons for climbing the mountain was a curious one, suggested by I. Spassky-Avtonomov, another of the early climbers. They both wanted to ascertain whether the stars and planets are visible during the day from extremely high mountaintops.

Prior to the "modern" investigations, which started in the 1820s, there have been a number of hearsay or legendary accounts of ascents to the upper regions of Ararat and the sighting or touching of the Ark. These accounts concern visits to the Ark by holy men looking for sacred relics, herders searching for lost animals from their flocks, or collectors of wood or pitch from the ship at a time when the Ark was presumably accessible, as it possibly was before the last earthquake and eruption of Mount Ararat in 1840. These have been variously considered either as miracles or unusual exploits. In one case a shepherd told of finding a great cliff on the heights while he was searching for lost sheep. As he came closer to the presumed cliff, it turned out to be the side of an enormous ship partially covered by ice and snow, from which he fled in fear of punishment for his sacrilege.

But, in former times as now, shepherds have tended to avoid the extreme heights as a place of sickness and death, not realizing that the sickness is simply the mountain sickness induced by altitude. They recognize the danger zone as the point where "the sheep begin to die" and feel, understandably, that they have gone far enough.

According to tradition one Byzantine prelate attempted to climb to the Ark. This was a monk, Jacob of Medzpin, later Bishop of Nisbis, and finally a saint. After a long series of prayers to God that he be allowed to see the Ark, Jacob started a long climb up the west side of Mount Ararat. Tormented by thirst and overcome by fatigue, he lay down to rest. When he awoke he found that a spring had miraculously appeared near where he had rested. The spring, now called Jacob's Well, is still there and serves as a landmark on the mountain. Later he continued his climb but, after each rest, he would find upon waking that he was once again at the point where he had started, presumably carried down by angels. But God finally granted his prayers and sent an angel to visit him. The angel told Jacob to cease his attempts to climb the forbidden mountain and gave him a piece of the Ark. The angel then informed Jacob that the Ark was forbidden territory for mankind until such time as God Himself should choose to reveal it.

Sir John Chardin, an early observer of Mount Ararat, in commenting on this miracle in 1356, observed:

22

*   *   *

Instead of its being a miracle that no one could
ever reach the top, I should rather deem it a great
miracle if anyone *did* reach its summit. . . . From
its halfway point to the peak it is perpetually
covered with snow, so that at all seasons it has the
appearance of a vast heap of snow.

A British ascent was made to the top of Mount
Ararat in 1856 by a group led by a veteran of the Cri-
mean War, Major Robert Stuart. During his climb he
found that his Kurdish guides came to a halt at a certain
place ". . . and refused to proceed any further, alleging
in justification ancestral tradition and the fear of tread-
ing on holy ground . . . and said that to scale the mountain is impossible and that any attempt of this kind
would be followed by the immediate displeasure of
heaven."

When several members of the British party
reached the summit, however, some among the reluc-
tant Kurds, as reported by Major Stuart, exclaimed:
"We had always thought . . . that Allah had made that
holy mountain inaccessible to man; many have tried to
ascend it, but no one has ever succeeded until you come,
and without any preparation walk straight up from the
base to the top. Allah be praised! we have heard strange
things of you, but now we see them with our own eyes."
The major apparently accepted this accolade with British aplomb and reported it in an entry worthy of the
best traditions of Empire: ". . . then indeed they began
to feel the force of what we asserted . . . that many
things forbidden to the Kurds are allowed to the English."

The northeastern part of Turkey is a frequent

scene of earthquakes and has been so throughout recorded history. An especially violent earthquake occur-
ring in June 1840 completely demolished the town of
Arghuri (Ahora) located on the northeastern side of
Ararat. The earthquake and eruption of Mount Ararat
killed all of Ahora's inhabitants and also destroyed the
Armenian monastery of St. Jacob, once visited by Parrot
and other travelers, that was reputed to contain a
number of ancient records pertaining to the Ark as well
as pieces of the Ark itself. The event left a deep gorge at
the melting end of the Black Glacier, so called because
of the covering of black dust coming from the crushed
shattered rocks. This dropoff, almost 800 feet of sheer
cliff, is called the Ahora Gorge. At the bottom of the
gorge water collects from the seasonally melting bottom
of the 600-foot-thick glacier directly above the gorge.

It would seem normal to suppose that if the Ark
had really survived thousands of years on the mountain
it would either have been exposed by the above-men-
tioned seismic disaster or been itself demolished. But
subterranean, submarine, or subglacial results of an
earthquake are rarely predictable, and a reported discovery of the Ark by Turkish authorities was not made
public until the summer of 1883 when a new earthquake had shaken the mountain and demolished a
number of villages.

The Turkish commissioners, including an attaché
of the British Embassy at Istanbul (then Constantinople)
were assessing the damages and changes when they reportedly came upon a huge wooden boatlike structure.
It was painted brown, made of heavy timbers, some of
which were broken, and the end of it emerged from the
bottom of an overhanging glacier. The commissioners
estimated the height of the object to be fifty feet, its

length the equivalent of 300 cubits, and reported that they actually entered the shiplike structure. They were able to penetrate three large compartments but the other sections were filled with solid ice. After reassessing their situation they prudently decided to abandon the investigation of their find because of the possibility that the huge glacial overhang might collapse on the ship and on themselves as well.

This report concerning the Ark first appeared in the press of Constantinople and soon thereafter in the *Levant Herald* and the British *Prophetic Messenger*. But, instead of awakening scientific or archaeological interest in the Ark legend, it furnished the American press with an item ready made for the kind of reporting reserved for UFO stories of a later day. The *New York Herald* noted that, since a British officer was among the discoverers, the height of the stalls on board the presumed vessel was in accord with the "specifications of the British Admiralty [for horse transport] and therefore not open to doubt." As for the length of the craft—300 cubits—"a nation that has seriously thought of a ship railway across Central America can not doubt that the Ark can be brought to deep water," adding that when such a thing happened and the Ark "reaches American waters . . . the Navy Department ought to purchase her at once, for the world's greatest republic ought to have at least one ship that will not rot as soon as it leaves a navy yard. . . ."

An article in the *Chicago Tribune* reported that the inhabitants in the vicinity of Ararat had noted the great structure of dark wood for some years but had been afraid to go near it ". . . because a spirit of fierce aspect had been seen looking out of the window." The official party, it stated, had recognized the Ark immediately since ". . . there was an Englishman among them who had presumably read his Bible and he saw that it was made of the ancient gopherwood of scripture. . . " (a gratuitous quip since "gopherwood" is still not satisfactorily identified).

A feature writer of the *New York World* changed the nationality of the exploring party to Russians and then compared the finding of the Ark to the famous Cardiff Giant hoax. He added, ". . . the reader must not be surprised [if he learns] from the latest dispatches from our representative, Mr. Benjamin, that the engineers have broken through the third compartment of the Ark and in the true spirit of the age have discovered the original log kept by Noah and his sons. . . ."

As in the case of today's press reporting of UFO sightings, no follow-ups appeared in the newspapers, and the entire incident was more or less forgotten—except for the readers' impression that something of a hoax had been perpetrated.

It was in this atmosphere that another series of curious incidents took place, only four years after the reported post-earthquake discovery. This time it concerned a report made to the World Parliament of Religions, meeting in Chicago in 1893, by a John Joseph, Prince of Nouri, who held, among numerous other titles, that of Archbishop and Grand Apostolic Ambassador of Malabar, India, and Persia. Prince Nouri stated at the meeting that he had reached the Ark during his explorations in 1887 to ascertain the source of the Euphrates. He claimed to have tried to climb Mount Ararat three times, succeeding on the third attempt. He described the Ark as being more than 100 feet high and 300 yards long, with one end broken off. Following the considerable publicity caused by his statements, he undertook to organize an expedition to Mount Ararat and to lead it up to the point where the Ark was lying, and then to disassemble the Ark for easier transportation and to reassemble it for exhibition at the then current Chicago World's Fair. To this end he successfully involved a group of investors, but the enterprise was halted practically at its inception since Turkish permission for the undertaking was denied.

Prince Nouri's career, further complicated by his being mugged while on a trip to San Francisco, and a resultant stay in a mental hospital, came to an untimely end in the early 1900s, leaving unresolved further verification of his discovery of the Ark.

The difficulty of proving the existence of a ship on or near the summit of Ararat has been compounded by the lack of photographs and contemporaneous corroboration from other witnesses. A number of reports of individual visits to the Ark in the nineteenth century (see Chapter 6) did not surface until after the second decade of the twentieth century when a striking event concerning the Ark occurred during World War I. A variety of contemporary and corroborative reports of this incident and its subsequent ramifications are still circulating. Even now, new information from secondary witnesses is still being received, although the number of such witnesses becomes fewer each passing year.

3

Aircraft and the Ark

An unusual sighting of the Ark, and perhaps the most celebrated, allegedly occurred in the summer of 1916, during the thaw. It was made by a Lieutenant Roskovitsky and his copilot while flying an observation airplane of the Russian Imperial Air Force. Their orders were to accomplish high-altitude tests and also to observe Turkish troop movements during a time when the Russian armies were being hard pressed on several fronts. Their small air base was located about twenty-five miles northeast of Mount Ararat. Roskovitsky and his copilot, equipped with oxygen tanks for high-altitude breathing, approached Mount Ararat from the northeast, circled it twice and then, as it got closer, Roskovitsky noticed a half-frozen lake on a shelf or gully on the side of the mountain, similar to those glacial concentrations which increase or decrease in size according to seasonal glacial melting.

As they flew nearer, the copilot pointed to something near the lake's overflow and Roskovitsky realized that he was looking at what appeared to be a half submerged hull of some sort of huge ship. At first he thought that it might be a submarine, unconsciously attributing to the Germans, masters of submarine warfare, the ability to launch a submarine within a lake well up on the side of a massive mountain. He then noticed that what he first took for periscopes were two stubby masts and that the ship, which it apparently was, was leaning to one side, into the ice. He also noticed a flat catwalk down the length of the top of the ship.

In Roskovitsky's words (from the *New Eden Magazine*, California, 1939): "We flew down as close as safety permitted and took several circles around it. We were surprised when we got close to it, at the immense size of the thing, for it was as long as a city block, and would compare very favorably in size to the modern battleships of today. It was grounded on the shore of the lake, with one-fourth underwater. It had been partly dismantled on one side near the front, and on the other side there was a great doorway nearly twenty feet square, but with the other door gone. This seemed quite out of proportion, as even today, ships seldom have doors even half that large. . . ."

After this somewhat cursory examination Roskovitsky returned to his base and informed the base commander, a captain, of what he had seen. The captain, understandably impressed, told Roskovitsky to take him back to the site and told him after seeing it that what he had flown over was Noah's Ark, explaining its survival by the supposition that it was "frozen up for nine or ten months of the year, it couldn't rot, and has been in cold storage, as it were, all this time. . . ."

The captain forwarded a report back to St. Petersburg with the result that orders came from the Tsar to send two engineer companies up the mountain. One group of fifty men attacked one side, and the other group of one hundred men attacked the big mountain from the other side. Two weeks of hard work were required to chop out a trail along the cliffs of the lower part of the mountain, and it was nearly a month before the Ark was reached.

> *That the Imperial Government, by order of the Tsar, should send specialized troops to climb up Mount Ararat during a time they were needed elsewhere raises the possibility of a psychological operation planned to give the Russian Army and people a spiritual uplift and indications of divine protection in the dark days prior to the February (or March, in the new calendar) Revolution which overthrew the Tsar. (The Germans had previously attempted religio-psychological operations including powerful airborne magic lanterns projecting onto cloud banks over the German lines pictures of the Holy Family and Russian saints who seemed to hover protectively over the German trenches.)*

Complete measurements were taken, and plans drawn of it, as well as many photographs, all of which were sent to the Tsar. The magazine article proceeds:

The Ark was found to contain hundreds of small rooms, and some rooms that were very large, with high ceilings. The unusually large rooms had a fence of great timbers across them, some of which were two feet thick, as if designed to hold beasts ten times the size of elephants. Other rooms were also lined with tiers of cages, somewhat like what one sees today at a poultry show, only instead of chicken wire, they had rows of small iron bars along the front.

*   *   *

The writer of the article, by mentioning "beasts ten times as large as elephants" (dinosaurs inside the Ark?) tends here to destroy his credibility. If, on the other hand, the Roskovitsky story, written long after the event, is a compendium of a variety of witnesses—pilots, soldiers, engineers, etc.—it is understandable that exaggerations should occur.

Everything was heavily painted with a waxlike paint resembling shellac, and the workmanship of the craft showed all the signs of a high type of civilization. The wood used throughout was oleander, which belongs to the cypress family and never rots; which of course, coupled with the fact of its being frozen most of the time, accounted for its perfect preservation.

The above seems so close to the Biblical description that André Parrot (see Bibliography), a French writer on the Ark and the Flood, dismissed Roskovitsky's whole account with: ". . . It is most unfortunate that no competent person saw this report . . . lost during the course of the Bolshevist Revolution of 1917. All we have is Roskovitsky's story, of which the least that can be said is that if it is shorn of reminiscences of Genesis, scarcely anything is left. . . . That did not prevent several American periodicals from proclaiming the sensational news. Serious specialized organs reserved for it the fate it deserved: silence. . . ."

. . . The expedition found on the peak of the mountain above the ship the remains of the timbers which were missing out of one side of the ship. It seemed that these timbers had been hauled up to the top of the peak, and used to build a tiny shrine. . . .

This mention of a shrine is an especially intriguing feature of the Roskovitsky account in that it seems to explain why separate timbers have been found at different points at the highest levels of the mountain, thousands of feet above the tree line. If, during the thousands of years that the ship had lain on the mountain and had been visited by occasional pilgrims, at a time when it was more visible and more accessible, some of them would probably have constructed a shrine near or at the summit, made out of the Ark's wood, in remembrance perhaps of the traditional atlar built by Noah after the Flood.

Roskovitsky's published account breaks off rather abruptly, simply stating that the investigative officers sent photographs and reports by courier back to Petrograd, to the personal attention of the Tsar. But Nicholas II apparently never received them during the breakdown of communications that followed the February and October Revolutions of 1917.

The results of the investigation have either never been found or never been reported. A rumor exists that the results of the investigation and the pictures of the Ark came to the attention of Leon Trotsky, who either destroyed them or placed them in a file destined to be kept permanently secret. According to the same rumor, the special courier's silence on the matter was also permanently secured by his execution.

*　　*　　*

Roskovitsky's account ends with the simple statement that he and several other pilots escaped the Bolsheviki via Armenia and eventually arrived in America.

An enigma and stumbling block in the acceptance of this much published report, however, lies in the identity of Roskovitsky: no known survivor of the Imperial Army or Air Force in the Ararat area at that time remembers any Lieutenant Roskovitsky. This would seem to indicate that he never existed or that at the time that he wrote the magazine article, even though it was twenty-two years after his discovery of the Ark, he was unwilling to use his own name for reasons of self-protection—even in America.

Nevertheless there has been considerable recollection among individual Russian Army survivors who were involved in operations during that period and in that locale. Eryl Cummings, an outstanding researcher of the Ark legend for more than forty years and veteran of twenty-five ascents of Ararat, was able to make personal contact with a Colonel Alexander Koor, author of an article about the incident printed in 1945 in *Rossiya* an overseas Russian magazine, in New York. Colonel Koor had been in command of the 19th Petropavlovsky Regiment, stationed near Mount Ararat in 1915–1916 with the mission of protecting the Aratsky Pass at a time that Turkish forces had made a partial breakthrough in the Russian lines. Colonel Koor remembered having heard of the reputed finding of the Ark and gave pertinent information in a certified interview with Ark researcher Eryl Cummings.

Colonel Koor stated that it was his opinion that

the pilot who viewed the Ark was First Lieutenant Zabolotsky, and the captain's name, not given in the original article, was Kurbatov. Zabolotsky, according to Colonel Koor, sighted the Ark and started the investigation. Koor had spoken to a Lieutenant Piotr Leslin in 1921, who informed him that he, Leslin, had heard about the discovery "not as a rumor but as news" told to him by the senior adjutant of his division and that ". . . Noah's Ark was found in the saddle of the two peaks of Ararat."

Koor also supplied information about the later visit to the Ark by the engineer battalion which he received from Boris Rujansky, a family friend who in 1916–1917 was a sergeant of the Military Railroad Battalion, then stationed near Doğubayazit, located several miles from Mount Ararat and through which the railroad formerly passed. Sergeant Rujansky had actually taken part in the investigation and corroborated the ascent of the battalion to the heights of Mount Ararat.

The Koor account was more complete than the Roskovitsky article in that it specified that one of the two investigative expeditions had climbed Ararat by following an existing trail. At one point they found that their climb had led them to a place where they were looking down on the huge ship which had one end underwater. The other unit, which arrived there first, did not follow a trail but had to cut steps in the ice as they climbed. When this unit reached the ship a number of the soldiers crossed themselves, some falling on their knees in prayer before entering it. Inside the Ark, according to the Koor article, there were partitions—it appeared there were also rust marks on the floor, presumably from the iron rods that marked the rusted iron bars of many small and some very large partitions.

Despite persistent efforts by Eryl Cummings, Dr. John Montgomery (*The Quest for Noah's Ark*), who also interviewed Colonel Koor in 1970, and others the official reports and photographs referred to in several versions of the 1916 discovery of the Ark have never surfaced to public view. But a number of interviews and statements have, including the separate testimonies of individual Russian soldiers who, during a maneuver around Mount Ararat in the summer of 1917, remember seeing a wooden structure shaped like a ship several hundred feet above them as they marched by. The soldiers noticed that one end of the object they saw went back into the snow and ice of the mountain.

The author has personal recollections of conversations with refugee Russian officers in Paris in the mid-1920s, officers who had left the Caucasus area with refugees from the armies of General Denikin, one of the last generals who held out against the Communists until there was no hope but retreat over the border and escape. Several of these officers had been active in Turkey and still remembered hearing a report about the finding of the Ark on Mount Ararat. The story had been retold through the armies on the southern front but was overshadowed by the fall of the dynasty and the disintegration of the Imperial armies.

Another unusual legend was current among Russian officers and their families. This was that several members of the Imperial Family had escaped the massacre at Ekaterinburg in 1918 and had been spirited away through a network of monasteries and convents to safety in other countries.

This sort of legend has occurred on various occasions in the stormy history of Imperial Russia. Russian history has witnessed a number of pretenders to the crown, "false" Tsars or "false" heirs to the throne, whose putative identity was usually settled by their defeat and execution. It was only natural that such legends have subsisted in regard to the last Imperial Family and certain survivors, notably Anastasia, the youngest Imperial Princess, as well as the Tsarevich, have been the subject of a number of books published in Great Britain and the United States. One alleged Tsarevich bearing the same name as the son of the last Tsar, Alexei Nikolaevich Romanov, and considered so by a number of people and personally convinced as well, was alive until May 1986 and living in Phoenix, Arizona. The author was able to locate him through the assistance of Violet Cummings, author of several books on the Ark (see Bibliography) and wife of Eryl Cummings, with the aim of ascertaining any memories that Alexei Romanov might have regarding the expedition to the Ark ordered by the Tsar.

The following excerpt is from the author's first telephone conversation with Alexei Nikolaevich Romanov. It is pointed out that Mr. Romanov was the same age as the Tsarevich would have been had he survived, and was in poor health at the time of the interview.

Question: Do you remember hearing about Noah's Ark being found on Mount Ararat in 1916?

Yes, I remember hearing talk about the discovery. A ship had been seen near the top of the mountain by aviators.

Who talked about it?

I heard about it from my father and people were talking about it in the palace.

* * *

Do you remember your father, the Emperor, saying he had sent an expedition to the place where the Ark was found?

Yes, something of that sort. My father consulted with the Duma and I think the Duma made the decision. Army officers had reported it. The army was in Turkey then. I remember my father saying that an expedition was sent.

Was that the Russian Army in the Caucasus under the command of the Grand Duke Nikolai Nikolaevich?

(With enthusiasm) That was my uncle! Do you know he was almost seven feet tall? He used to carry me sometimes. I used to see him at Tsarkoye-Selo. That's north of Petrograd. I don't remember much. I was very sick. . . .

Comment: *The above memories are offered only as a possible corroboration of the expedition to the Ark from someone who considered himself to be the son of Russia's last Emperor and may have been so or perhaps a relative. Other reminiscences from individuals who were at the Imperial Court in Petrograd have made similar statements about what they remembered having heard discussed.*

There are also memories among the Kurds and Turks. Mustafa, a former herdsman now living in Doğubayazit and whose present activities are centered in visits to the mosque and teahouse, is now over eighty-five years old. He was interviewed in August 1985 in order to ascertain if he had ever heard about the Russian expedition to find the Ark.

Mustafa said:

Yes, I remember one thing very well. My father was working on the railroad the Russians were repairing.

What people worked in the work teams?

The teams had Russians and also Turks and Kurds.

Did the teams hear anything about the Russian expedition?

By Allah! One day everybody did. It was in late summer, one afternoon. We heard a great noise of shooting and yelling *Hourrah!* by the Russians. In the village we thought it was a battle because the Russians always yell *Hourrah!* in attacks. Then my father came running in. I remember that it was early for him to come home. He told us it was no battle but that the Russians were drinking bottles of vodka and firing off rifles, revolvers, and one machine gun.

What did he say had happened?

He told us that the head of the team said to the workers, "Don't you know what happened on the mountain? They found the Ark! The team that was sent by the Tsar himself! It is a day of great joy for the Russians!"

Were you surprised?

It is as Allah wills. We always thought that the Ark was on Ağri Dağh but did not think the Russians would find it.

Where on the mountain did you hear they had found it?

Near Lake Küp. But the Russians left after a while. The Ark must still be there.

The Roskovitsky account and corroborative statements from a variety of sources have understandably been discounted as lacking in essential proof such as photographs, official reports, or certified substantiations. It is fruitless for defenders of these reports to point out that the disappearance of records and photographs would be a natural result of the ensuing revolution and civil war in Russia. Another influential factor would be the change in the religious temperament of the Russian people, from one of the world's most religious empires to an officially antireligious association of republics. This situation makes any investigation of a religious nature difficult, or even any investigation of an archaeological nature if connected with religion. Americans exploring Mount Ararat in search of the Ark, as well as flights of American aircraft in the vicinity of Mount Ararat, meet with suspicion and often protests from the Soviet side of the border where the impression is evident that American explorers have used the search for spying activities.

But whether the Roskovitsky report was true, false, or partially true, it has generated on its own the most definite source in centuries toward a reappraisal of the Ark legend. It is noteworthy that it was only *after* 1916–1917 that a number of sightings of the Ark previous to 1916 became public. These have included a number of personal visits to the Ark, the bringing back of worked planks and timbers found at high altitudes where there was no wood, and even deathbed confessions from one person who had been afraid to tell of his experiences and others who had attempted to discredit the Ark's existence after seeing it (Chapter 6).

Many of the subsequent visits to Ararat have been encouraged and inspired by other sightings from the air during the period between the wars, during World War II, and thereafter. As far as can be ascertained, none of these air probes, by military aircraft, helicopter, satellites, or space shuttles have been looking for the Ark but, in some cases, have come across it unexpectedly or have found a shiplike profile outlined in a photograph. Photographs from the air or from space have reportedly shown a great ship on the side of the mountain but no definite or identifiable photograph of a wooden ship on Mount Ararat has as yet been made available to the public.

During the military-supply operation between the USA and the USSR in World War II, considerable air traffic developed between the main US base in Tunisia and the Russian base at Erivan in the Armenian SSR. It was during 1943 that two American pilots, flying near Mount Ararat, thought they saw something resembling the outline of a great ship thousands of feet below them. Upon retracing their earlier flight they were accompanied by an Air Corps photographer who took a picture of it, subsequently published according to a number of witnesses on the front page of the Mediterranean edition of *Stars and Stripes,* the US Armed Forces newspaper. This *Stars and Stripes* photo is only one of a number of pictures allegedly taken of the Ark during World War II by US, Australian, and especially Russian airmen. A number of people remember seeing them, but the photographs share a common feature—they cannot be produced. Some Russian pilots have reportedly shown pictures of a large ship on an ice-covered mountain to Allied airmen during the period of the munitions airlift from the south, alleging that it was a photograph of the Ark. But the Russian pilots, in all cases, have refused to let the pictures out of their hands, an understandable refusal considering the active anti-religious policy of the Soviet regime. The photographs taken by American pilots also seem to have vanished, even the one published by *Stars and Stripes,* lost somewhere among the old files of the Mediterranean editions of 1943. All things considered, it may be that the *Stars and Stripes* photograph was a picture of a volcanic rock formation not on Mount Ararat but almost twenty miles away which, somewhat surprisingly, *does* possess the approximate shape and dimensions of the Ark of legend (see Chapter 4).

A number of American pilots saw a shiplike construction protruding from the side of Mount Ararat in the late spring or summer of 1960. These pilots were based at Adana, Turkey, with the 428th Tactical Flight Squadron under the NATO Military Assistance Pact in effect at that time. The pilots had been told about the Ark by the Turkish liaison pilot assigned to them and on several occasions had been guided past Mount Ararat on routine observation flights. These pilots did not have time to make any successful photographs because of their haste to make a quick turn around the mountain before becoming an object of unusual interest by Russian observers on the USSR side of the border.

Captain (then Second Lieutenant) Gregor Schwinghammer, now a commercial pilot, was interviewed by the author in 1981 concerning a bargelike object he had seen on Mount Ararat as described in *Doomsday, 1999 A.D.* He stated that the Turkish liaison officer had accompanied him and another pilot in a counterclockwise swing around Mount Ararat in the course of which they saw "an enormous boxcar or rectangular barge visible in a gully high on the mountain." Captain Schwinghammer specified that it seemed to be banked, indicating that it was not stationary but movable and somehow had become caught there as it slid down the mountain. He remembered that he had later heard at the base club that some pictures had been taken of this object, reputedly by the U-2 pilots prior to the unexpectedly sudden ending of the U-2 program when Gary Powers was brought down over the USSR and captured by Soviet air action.

The author, after returning from his own investigative trip to the Ararat area in August 1985, again interviewed Captain Schwinghammer and other former pilots of the 428th Tactical Flight Squadron to ascertain whether some of his memories of the icebound ship on Ararat coincided with other subsequent sightings.

Question: What did the other pilots think about what you and they had seen?

We used to talk about it in the bar after flying. Some of the pilots thought it was the Ark and others didn't know what to think. I was not convinced about that but I knew that I had seen a large rectangular building like a barge or a ship high up on the mountain.

How far away from the object were you when you saw it?

We were coming down from 5000 feet. I think we were at more like 3000 feet when we sighted it. I remember that we were doing 380 knots. The

Turkish liaison pilot said to us, "That's where Noah's Ark is supposed to be. Look! You can see it now!" I estimate that I saw it at a 45° angle. It appeared to be hanging at 45° or 30° degrees down the mountain.

Did you take any photographs of it?

No. We were in too much of a hurry. We had two hours of fuel; it took us forty-five minutes to get there in the F-100. We had time enough to make just one pass around the mountain and return. We had to be very careful. The Russians had a radar installation right on the border. A C-130 had recently been shot down. The pilot was a guy named Dick Skiddip.

From your memory, where was the object on the mountain?

You can tell approximately from the map. The point where I place the Ark we saw was about 4000 feet from the top on the southeast slope, perhaps four o'clock from due north.

Do you think it would still be visible?

I think most of the time it is covered with ice and snow and that we just saw it at a time when part of it was protruding from the snow. I know that I saw a rectangular structure that looked like a ship. It was at a period in time or history and we were there at that time.

Other pilots in the squadron remember having taken part in flights over Ararat or having heard that other pilots had seen a shiplike object on the mountain.

44

Lieutenant Colonel Ben Bowthorp (then a first lieutenant):

> I was the deputy base commander at the time. Greg [Schwinghammer] was there at the same time. A Turkish pilot told us that the Ark was on the side of the mountain. It seemed logical to me. We took a bunch of flights around the area, looking at castles and ruins, and then on Ararat we saw something different. It was about two-thirds of the way up the mountain, made of wood, and it looked like a boat or a wooden boat-shaped wall. I don't know who first said it was Noah's Ark. We all discussed it. Most of us felt it could be, since that's where it's supposed to be.

Captain Lloyd Hawkins:

> I was assistant squadron commander and heard about the incident at the time that it happened. I did not put too much faith in it at the time, but I clearly remember hearing about some pilots seeing something unusual on the mountain.

Colonel Robert Phillips (then first lieutenant):

> I was rotated through Adana with another squadron. I heard rumors, talking to people at the bar, about some of the pilots having seen the outline of something looking like a big ship or a barge on the mountain. I didn't get a chance to see it because they told us to steer clear of Ararat—not to go near it because of what happened to the U-2.

Colonel J. L. Pennington (then first lieutenant):

> We used to go on trips from time to time and sometimes we went hunting for wild boars. I do recall that some pilots in the squadron said they had seen Noah's Ark. But that was so long ago. . . .

Colonel Bradley Tellshaw (then second lieutenant):
I was on one of the flights in the area. I remember
seeing something—an unusual outline on the
mountain, but I could not be sure what it was.

People who think they have seen the Ark have occasionally made sketches of it or instructed artists how
to draw what they had seen. An unusual coincidence
occurred when William Crouse, Ararat explorer and
senior minister of Probe Ministries, sent Captain
Schwinghammer a booklet called *The Search for Noah's
Ark* (J. Bitzer, Probe Ministries: 1985) describing search
activities on Ararat and difficulties encountered in
1985. The booklet contained a sketch of the Ark made
by Elfred Lee, a longtime Ararat explorer, under the
direction of an eyewitness. The witness, an Armenian
named George Hagopian, an ex-shepherd, claimed to
have climbed up to the Ark in 1905 at the age of ten and
to have seen it on several other occasions. According to
Hagopian he had even walked along the roof of the
giant ship.
Schwinghammer, who had never previously seen
the picture "dictated" to Lee, had independently asked
one of his acquaintances to draw a picture of what he,
Schwinghammer, had seen. The two pictures were essentially the same—the Ark banked in the snow, the
position of an outcropping of the mountain, and even
the shape of the barge or ship with the exception of
openings along the top of the structure, seen from the
ground but too small to have been visible from the aircraft. The pilot and the shepherd, unknown to each
other, had seen and described the same icebound ship,
evidently at a time that it was partially visible outside the
ice.

Although it is intriguing to find that separate viewers have sketched similar pictures of the Ark, the lack of photographs and the fact that photographs have subsequently disappeared is a recurring disappointment to researchers of the great ship.

Some of the mysterious disappearances of photographs lend a James Bond flavor to Ark investigation. In 1952 an oil engineer named George Jefferson Greene, a passenger in a helicopter reconnaissance flight for an oil company, flew around Mount Ararat. Greene suddenly noticed what seemed to be a large prow of a ship emerging from the ice. This was on the northeast side of the mountain, where so many sight-

Route of Lieutenant Schwinghammer around Ararat in an F-100 aircraft, showing the side of the mountain near the Ahora Gorge where he sighted a shiplike formation. *Drawing © 1986, Ahmet Ali Arslan*

ings have occurred. On Greene's orders the pilot maneuvered the helicopter to points as close as 100 feet from the object, during which time Greene excitedly used up a roll of film on the unusual object. When Greene developed the photographs he found that they showed a shiplike form located in a gully between a high cliff wall and a precipice, partially receding into the snow or glacier in back of it. In other words, essentially the description and situation given by other viewers. Allegedly the pictures had been taken from a close enough distance to show laminated planks on the ship's hull.

Greene made a number of prints and showed them to acquaintances in an attempt to obtain backing for his own expedition to Ararat. According to Ark researcher Eryl Cummings, Greene was not successful and the expedition did not take place.

Later Greene went to British Guyana to work with a mining company. He was murdered there in 1962, presumably in a robbery. His valuables, which may have included the close-up photographs of the Ark, were never located. Although a number of persons who stated that they had seen Greene's photographs were contacted by Cummings, no copy of any of the photographs has ever been located.

With the use of space satellites and space shuttles and their detailed inspection of much of the earth's surface, it could be hoped that some photographs of Mount Ararat would reveal information about the presence of the Ark, especially at the points where viewers have claimed to have seen it. One photograph taken from space in 1974 by Earth Research Technical Satellite (ERTS) revealed, after intensive enlargement, an unusual feature on the side of the mountain at the high altitude of 14,000 feet. The ERTS photograph was discussed by Senator Frank E. Moss, then chairman of the Senate Aeronautical and Space Sciences Committee, in a speech made to the Utah Section of the American Congress on Surveying and Mapping. He stated that an unusual object in one of the folds of the mountain "was about the right size and shape to be the Ark." The section of the mountain photographed was shot at an altitude of 450 to 500 miles, and the area is similar to the type of crevasse in the side of the mountain where the Ark or some other unusual construction has been seen by pilots. But any object seen from that height, as well as being half under the snow or in the shadow of a crevasse, would be almost impossible to identify even under extreme enlargement.

One thing is certain however. Whatever it is is not an optical illusion, which can come easily to straining eyes but not to sophisticated cameras. Future air inspection of Mount Ararat, especially during the late summer melting of the ice, and preferably by helicopter, might reveal the hidden ship in the upper region of the mountain, where a number of people claim to have seen it, approached it, and even touched it.

Despite the lack of clear or attainable photographs of the Ark on Mount Ararat there already exist numerous photographs of a suspected Ark located within twenty miles of Mount Ararat on another smaller range of mountains. This "alternate" ark bears a surprising resemblance to the Biblical description of the Ark and unlike the presumed Ark on Ararat it can be visited and photographed (provided one has local permission) by the relatively simple expedient of taking a taxi from Doğubayazit to the site on Akyayla Range. Since its discovery in 1959, and especially after the furor in the press and television within the last two years, it is well known. It has been theorized that this alternate Ark has either been fossilized so that it blends with the terrain or has been buried by mud slides. To differentiate it from the possible Ark on Mount Ararat it could best be described as the "buried" ship or ark near the Tendürek Mountains, the subject of the following chapter.

4

Volcanic Mound or Tomb of the Ark?

Those who belong to the "Peoples of the Book" (Jews, Christians, Moslems) have been conditioned since childhood to the acceptance of the legend of the Ark. This legend, if legend it be, is more persuasive than some other Old Testament stories such as Jonah and the whale, the snake in the Garden of Eden, and the extreme ages of the earth's early patriarchs. For the mountains of Ararat are still there and for thousands of years people have been hearing about Noah's Ark. Therefore almost any unusual feature of the mountain is likely to be associated with the Ark by observers from the air, the plain, or the nearby hills. These observers, even if they do not realize it, are psychologically conditioned to believe in its reality.

A discovery in 1959 was the result of a routine aerial survey taken near Ararat by the Turkish Air Force. The photographs taken by the pilot, Lieutenant A. Kurtis, at a ground altitude of 10,000 feet, were sent to headquarters where they were examined by a captain assigned to photo interpretation. One particular photograph caught his attention: unique because it showed a long oval hill smooth in form in an area that otherwise was marked with crevasses and gullies. The hill-like form seemed to be bounded by a raised ridge. The photograph was taken about seventeen miles south of Mount Ararat. Ararat! As he stared the captain realized that the oval hill was shaped like a ship. Its raised sides seemed to resemble a ship's gunwales and the prow was pointed toward the Tendürek peaks. The captain wondered what were the dimensions of this strange formation as he remembered the well-known instructions traditionally given by God to Noah: "The length of the Ark shall be three-hundred cubits, the breadth of it fifty cubits, and the height of it thirty cubits."

The dimensions of the strange hillock, measured by Turkish engineers during a two-day survey, showed the length of the "Ark" to be 500 feet, the width at the middle 150 feet, and the height of the gunwales 45 feet. These could be said roughly to correspond with the Biblical measurements of the Ark *if* we consider that the sides of the Ark could have split during the many intervening centuries, while the strong wooden planks of the hull still held their shape. Thus they would capture mud slides, stones, lava deposits, and still preserve their contours, clearly outlined against the rough terrain around them. Even the height would be increased on one side, as it is, in an area known for earth slides, lava streams, and seismic activity, as mud packed together with stones built up against the "ship's" walls and solidified. But where was the Ark? The first Turkish team found no trace of any construction. If the Ark were there it was buried underneath its facsimile, which would serve as its tomb.

An expedition formed by scientists and searchers from the United States, under the aegis of Turkish officers and therefore a Turkish expedition, examined the "Ark" hillock in the early summer of 1960. Its members included Professor Arthur Brandenberger, a photogrammetric specialist from Ohio State College; Dr. Siegfried, an archaeologist from the Chicago Oriental Institute; René Noorbergen, international correspondent and author; businessmen Hal Thompson and William Bishop; George Vandeman, explorer and searcher for the Ark and leader of the expedition; Turkish officers Major Maykal and Captain Durupinar, the air photography interpretation specialist who had originally noticed the phenomenon; and selected officers and men of the 3rd Cavalry Regiment of the Turkish Army. The presence of businessmen or simply believers in the Ark backing the expedition has been the general case in the many subsequent expeditions to the mountain.

In this regard the search for the Ark belongs in a category distinct from other treasure searches. There is no gold or treasure to be found and divided, as in the case of lost Spanish treasure fleets, lost cities in the jungle, treasures from ancient tombs, lost gold and silver mines, or buried pirate treasure. Except for the reported plan of Archbishop Nouri to bring the Ark down from the mountain and exhibit it at the Chicago World's Fair, the search for the Ark has had primarily a spiritual and secondarily an archaeological motive. When one meets searchers for the Ark one is impressed by their faith and the strength of their desire to prove the Ark is there.

The detailed examination effected by the expedition verified measurements roughly equivalent to those mentioned in the Bible. Some variations could be allowed for according to the accepted length of the cubit.

Also, the somewhat excessive width of the object could be explained by the splitting of the gunwales as the Ark filled with earth and was covered by lava and then more earth on top of that.

After some discussion among members of the expedition, the decision was reached (not unanimously, one assumes, considering the presence of the accompanying archaeologist) to dynamite a portion of the supposed Ark to see whether there existed evidence of wood or metal construction, remnants of pitch or stout inner timbers, in conformity with reports or legendary memories of Noah's Ark. Dynamite charges were placed and exploded by soldiers of the military escort and no inner chambers or clear evidence of beams were discovered although it was later claimed that bits of decayed wood were found among the debris.

It appeared and later was generally accepted that the "phantom" Ark was simply a natural uplift of the earth in an area of seismic activity; that it was solidified mud or lava—not the Ark or even a cast of the Ark. Nonetheless the pile of lava and earth bore a surprising resemblance to what one might visualize to be the hull of an ancient ship on the ocean floor, except that here was no ocean, only the memory of the sea, recalled by shells and sea fossils on and under the earth and on the mountain.

The simulacrum of the Ark remained relatively unnoticed from 1960 to 1984, during which time a number of explorers, mountaineers, and dedicated searchers for the Ark continued their expeditions on Mount Ararat itself.

Meanwhile a number of photographs of the phantom Ark appeared from time to time in the more sensational weekly newspapers, usually reproducing the

Turkish photograph of 1959, sometimes reinforced with heavy touching up of the original picture, which was attributed to aerial photographs by Turkish or Russian pilots.

In 1984 the buried Ark enjoyed a resurgence of publicity widely reported in the world press. This came as a result of an expedition which visited and inspected the object and collected from it specimens of stone, lava, and soil. This team was headed by Marvin Steffins, president of International Explorations, and Ronald Wyatt, an anesthetist who had visited the site in previous years.

Upon returning to Ankara, Steffins announced that the boat-shaped formation was indeed the Ark and that he had taken a number of samples from the formation and had packed them in sacks. These samples consisted of wood, soil, and stones to be analyzed upon his return to the United States. Wyatt had also taken some samples which he planned to have analyzed in Knoxville, Tennessee.

As the removal of any valuable antique (an understated but apt description of the Ark) is likely to provoke a negative response from any national government where the antiques are found, the Turkish government soon heard about the sacks and intercepted Steffins at the Istanbul airport as he was leaving Turkey. But it was not contraband, simply 8.6 pounds of stones, sand, and earth, innocent enough but still officially Turkish property. In the meantime Wyatt had taken his own collection to New York and exhibited it at a press conference. This appropriation of national property elicited considerable press reaction in Turkey. One editorial in the English-language *Turkish Times* attacked not only the taking of samples but the lack of consideration by foreigners for the customs and regulations of the nation, adding, in an adroit reference to the Flood legend, "without these considerations we degenerate to the level of uncivilized beings that God sent the Flood to the world to destroy."

The incident, which interrupted other expeditions on the mountain as well, soon developed an other-worldly aspect. Colonel Irwin, the famous astronaut who had walked on the moon, had in his luggage a replica of moon rock he had collected from the moon's surface. This rock was also seized by officials for exam-ination as a possible illegal export from Turkey until Colonel Irwin explained that it was not archaeological and not of Turkish origin and, indeed, not of this world.

A new investigation of the phantom Ark took place in March 1985. This time an improved prototype of molecular-frequency scanner was used in order to de-tect whether there was a bulk shape or metal within the mound. The molecular-frequency scanner operates on the same principle as the CAT scanner used in hospitals to locate and measure foreign growths within the organs of the human body. The scanner was brought to Turkey by David Fasold, a longtime student of the Ark and an enthusiastic believer in its actual existence, not on the top of Great Ararat but on a smaller range eigh-teen miles away. Fasold is an ex-merchant marine of-ficer (with a master's license) and an experienced underwater diver and salvor who has long worked with side-scanning subsurface radar for identifying under-water wrecks. He is more familiar with the sea than with mountains but convinced, as he says, that whether un-derwater or under earth, "I know a ship when I see one."

Fasold and Wyatt visited the buried Ark in March, fighting their way through the deep snow. Fasold had brought the scanner with him and he determined to their mutual satisfaction that there was a massive bulk or some sort of object under the snow and inside the mound. Indications of iron showed up in traceable lines crisscrossed by other lines at definite intervals. Faced with this information Wyatt was immediately convinced that the Ark had been found and suggested that the iron indicated remains of great nails used for fastening beams or perhaps the bars of animal cages.

When they stopped for food at a gas station restaurant on their way back to Ankara, local bus and truck drivers wanted to know how they came to be so snow-burned. Their car driver explained: "These Americans are heroes! They have a machine that has helped them discover the holy Ark." This somewhat premature statement called forth blessings, free food, and toasts of raki.

Fasold and Wyatt returned to Turkey in June with Dr. John Baumgardner, a NASA research scientist from Los Alamos. This time, unencumbered by snow, they identified nine traverse lines by following the metal dots, crossing thirteen long lines that seemingly outlined the hull of a giant ship, curved as a ship would be, not boxlike, with what would be the keel line bearing ten degrees north toward Mount Ararat.

It was thereupon decided that Fasold would return to the United States to pick up a high-tech interface radar unit (also used by NASA), rented by him from Geophysical Survey Systems, Inc., and bring it back to Turkey. Such a machine would be capable of photographing what the CAT scanner had merely indicated. It could penetrate fifty feet under the surface of the land and could clearly depict what was inside the Ark mound. Special permission for the use of this interface radar outside the US had to be obtained from NASA.

Permission also had to be granted by the Turkish government for its use inside Turkey.

During August, while the team waited for the unit to arrive, they began to reexamine the site. The group now included Wyatt; Baumgardner; Mahlon Wilson, who had brought a core-drilling machine; Tom Fenner, an exploratory geologist who was to run the interface radar; and George Hause, the photographer for the expedition. The previous experiment with the CAT scanner was repeated and after a number of probes a series of ribbons was strung over the phantom Ark ostensibly to follow direction lines which indicated concentration of metal. Orange ribbons were used to determine lines going from east to west and yellow ribbons crisscrossed these, going from north to south. When the ribbons were in place the outline made the object look more like a ship than ever. Some skeptics present have observed that, although at some instances the metal detector was not turned on, the lines continued to trace the figure of a ship. These first tests were psychologically aided by Ron Wyatt's running commentary to the press, television crew, and other observers. At one point, as he walked over the rise between the gunwales, he stated that he was standing over the captain's cabin and later made references to the tracing indicated by the ribbons as indicating iron bars marking the now buried ancient cages for the animals on the Ark.

Fasold returned to Doğubayazit with the subsurface interface radar recording unit and the necessary permits. But when he arrived he found that Ararat and the surrounding area had once more been declared off limits to foreign investigators because terrorists had captured several expeditions on the upper slopes, confiscated their equipment, and chased them off the mountain at gunpoint (see Chapter 5).

Although Turkish commandos soon dispersed and rounded up the insurgents the interdiction on Ark exploration remained. Fasold was therefore unable to operate the machine but renewed his efforts in the summer of 1986 (see Chapter 10). It should be observed that even if the radar recording unit does not eventually give positive proof of a buried ship beneath the shiplike mound, the unit could also be used on suspect areas on the mountain itself as it is equally effective in distinguishing forms, dimensions, and details of objects under snow, ice, or water, as well as those buried in the earth.

Fasold considers that the location of the buried Ark, seventeen miles from Mount Ararat, is compatible with the Koranic mention of Mount Judi as the resting place of the Ark, since Judi in Arabic means simply "the heights" and that it is also in keeping with Biblical tradition, which does not specifically say "Mount Ararat" but "the *mountains* of Ararat." Although the Tendürek Range is usually given as the site of the Ark mound, it is actually on the nearby Akyayla Range, which runs northwest and southeast fairly close to Doğubayazit. The section of hills where the Ark is located is referred to as Mahşer which means "doomsday"—a name reminiscent of events that, in the memory of many races, took place in the surrounding area.

The altitude of the object is 6300 feet above sea level, considerably lower than that estimated for the Ark on Ararat; but its present level, according to Fasold's theory, is the result of a sudden slide from a greater height in the Akyayla Range, where it had been situated since the Flood occurred. This slide down the mountain resulted in its being buried in mud and sand which, by a process of siliconization, petrified the giant ship and preserved its shape. It might have been stopped in its downward slide by a large rock formation which can still be seen piercing the side of the object or what would be the port bulwark of the ship. This buried Ark, Fasold contends, was not noticed before now because it was not at the place where the Ark was supposed to be. Since it was sighted from the air, however, earthquakes in the area have caused it to rise and the ground around it has eroded away, leaving the Ark shape more evident.

If the object is effectively proved to be part of a ship the claim that it is Noah's Ark would still be in some doubt. It is interesting to note that many of the local population know of the object but consider it not to be the ship of Noah, which is up on the mountain, but the ship of Malik Shah, a ruler of ancient times who used a very large ship on a lake which covered an extensive area around Ararat and which may have connected with other large bodies of water to the south and north. (A lake still exists on the Ararat plain, fed by underground streams from the melting ice coming from Great and Little Ararat).

During 1987 the buried Ark will be examined, it is planned, by Turkish archaeologists as well as by a number of Americans if they can obtain the necessary permission. Since the time it was first discovered, however, explorers have on one occasion dynamited it or tried to take away pieces of it for testing. Therefore the Turkish authorities are inclined to prohibit digging or dislodging pieces of the buried ship or any other vessel found on the mountain, lest like certain other archaeological remains in different countries, they be partially or wholly dismantled.

But Fasold is convinced that for proving the artifact's identity as a ship digging into it would not be necessary or even productive, as the artifact itself has changed its molecular composition through siliconization and is now solid. He says: "Do you know what interface radar is capable of? You could see inside the object without demolishing it. You would be able to see beams, partitions, decks and iron bars, perhaps in place."

If the "buried" formation proves to be a large ship, what about the other Ark so often reported seen on Mount Ararat and believed to be Noah's Ark since remote antiquity? Could there be *two* Arks or even more, considering the Islamic assertion that the Ark was on Mount Judi (*Cudi*), also in Turkey but to the south; another on Mount Nisir; still another, on Mount Demavand in Iran; and various other landing places of survival ships in different parts of the world?

Nevertheless it is the reported presence on Mount Ararat of the Ark of Noah that still holds the belief and imagination of many of the world's people. Its definite location on the mountain where it is supposed to be would be an event that could change the mood of the present world, modifying its religious, historical, geophysical, and even political concepts. This is perhaps why, besides an understandable zeal for knowledge and exploration, so many climbers on the mountain, in their desire to find it have faced danger and death, sometimes finding both.

5

Dikkat!—Danger!

Ararat is certainly one of the world's most impressive and beautiful mountains; impressive because it rises an abrupt 14,000 feet from a plain already 3000 feet high. It is beautiful because it stands alone, away from other mountains, and when the cloud cover lifts from the summit, often in the early morning and evening, its gigantic mass and snow-covered dome causes one to raise one's head in a sort of involuntary salute to its size, mystery, and connection with mankind's most famous legend.

Ararat, with its two peaks of Greater and Lesser Ararat, covers an area of more than 600 square miles. It is a volcano which last erupted in 1840 causing the disappearance of the village and monastery of Ahora on its northeastern side and the formation of a great gorge, 800 feet deep, where the village used to be. A number of glaciers come down the mountain, of which the Parrot Glacier and the Abich I and Abich II glaciers are the largest in extent and, in places, 200 feet thick. Ararat's ice cap covers about twenty square miles and is thickest in the declivity between the two peaks of Greater Ararat. The sides of the mountain contain a number of gorges in which explorers and pilots at different times have reported seeing what they believed to be the remains of Noah's Ark. Other sites on the mountain suggested as possible resting places for the Ark include locations above the new village of Ahora, or points underneath the glacier or still under the ice at the summit. It is not at present possible to look for the Ark at Ahora because of its proximity to the border of the USSR.

The present favorite departure point for Ark-hunting expeditions or climbing parties simply interested in ascending the famous mountain is the town of Doğubayazit (pronounced Doh-bayazit), which forms the southern point of an almost equidistant triangle between Greater Ararat to the north and Lesser Ararat to the southeast. The "season" for Doğubayazit expeditions is a short but crowded one, since only in mid and late summer are climbing conditions, especially the lack of snow at lower levels, favorable to the difficult ascent. At such a time the climber, in addition to the normal and special difficulties to be expected on Mount Ararat, also encounters a pleasant profusion of mountain flowers, flocks of sheep, horses, wild goats, friendly shepherds, and notably unfriendly dogs.

However, there are so many dangers connected with exploration of the mountain, some mysterious and others patently obvious, that one can understand that the Turkish word for Ararat, Ağri Dağh—"the Mountain of Pain"—is an appropriate description of it.

The author interviewed Ahmet Ali Arslan, mountaineer, photographer, artist, writer, and holder of a doctorate from Erzurum University, about the special dangers peculiar to Mount Ararat. Dr. Arslan can be considered to be well informed on the subject as he has climbed to the summit of Greater Ararat seventeen times out of a total of thirty-seven climbs on the mountain. He was born in Aralik on the north side of Mount

Great Ararat from the north showing west side of Ahora Gorge looking east, at this point 800 feet deep. Abich Glaciers I and II are seen from left to right. The left-hand side is covered by ash. On the right-hand slope horses can be seen. These are wild horses, capable of fighting wolves. *Ahmet Ali Arslan*

The Black Glacier, colored by ash. This is where the town and monastery of Arghuri were destroyed in the 1840 eruption. The town and monastery vanished into the gorge. *Ahmet Ali Arslan*

First light over Ararat. Mount Ararat is the highest point of Turkey and catches the first light of day on Turkish land. *Ahmet Ali Arslan*

Volcanic rock covered with ash. Because of its tendency to crumble, this feature offers special danger to climbers. If a climber frightens wild goats, their movement frequently causes rock avalanches and landslides. A rifle shot or a loud call can also release a rockslide. *Ahmet Ali Arslan*

A stratified rock formation which, seen from afar, could be, and has been, mistaken for Noah's Ark. This one is called Devil's Rock (*Şeytan Kayasi*). The photograph was taken from east to west on the lower slopes of Mount Ararat. *Ahmet Ali Arslan*

Mount Ararat as seen from the streets of Doğubayazit. Its size, precipitous rise, and the absence of other mountains in the immediate vicinity exerts a mystic pull on the minds of dwellers in the town and the travelers who come to it. *Jay Bitzer, Probe Ministries*

Interior of tent at nomad camp. The nomads on the mountain are, in general, hospitable and helpful except that it is sometimes difficult for climbers to discern the difference between nomads, bandits, or insurgents. If you don't carry a gun, they are usually friendly. *Ahmet Ali Arslan*

Shepherds bring their flocks no higher than an altitude of 8000 feet. After that they note that the sheep begin to die, a phenomenon formerly believed to be because of the Divine interdiction against climbing the mountain. *Ahmet Ali Arslan*

Mount Ararat seen from Igdir, on the side of the mountain that is contiguous to the USSR. When you come to the village of Igdir, less than 2500 feet above sea level, the view of Ararat comes like a shock to the senses. There is nothing in view except the huge mountain; a presence so overwhelming that the visions generations of people have thought to see there are understandable. *Ahmet Ali Arslan*

Lesser Ararat as seen from the eastern slopes of Great Ararat at Mıh Tepe (Nail Head). The eastern part of Lesser Ararat touches the Iranian border where a lively commerce in arms is carried on. *Ahmet Ali Arslan*

Clouds lifting from Mount Ararat in a great funnel shape in the early evening. At this time, and when the sky is clear in the early morning, visitors for centuries have thought they saw the shape of an Ark high on the mountain, a phenomenon that has become more frequent with reports by pilots of having seen an Ark shape protruding from the snow in crevasses on the heights. *Jay Bitzer, Probe Ministries*

Early air view of buried Ark showing break in right side. Although claimed by many to be a natural formation, this shape has undoubtedly been the origin of some of the reports by pilots concerning sightings of the Ark. *The London Daily Telegraph*

Photostat of photograph of actual dynamiting of the buried Ark during the 1960 expedition (see Chapter 4) in an effort to ascertain whether the Ark shape contained pieces of wood. Some wood fragments were found. *René Noorbergen. (From files of the Society for the Investigation of the Unexplained.)*

Photograph from 1960 research expedition to the buried Ark shows investigators and Turkish mounted troops at the site. Walls of surrounding rim measured twenty feet high. *René Noorbergen*

Ararat and has been climbing the mountain since 1965. He has also had considerable climbing experience on the mountains of the Pamir Range located in the Kirghiz SSR.

Question: How do you, as an alpinist, rate Ararat in comparison with other mountains you have climbed?

Technically the climb is not too difficult. But it has been stated by scientists that there is active gas—carbon dioxide—on the upper slopes. This is in addition to the normal lack of oxygen on extreme heights. This combination is very hard on climbers and causes illness and confusion.

What about avalanches?

The snow avalanches are rare, except in spring when overhanging snow cliffs can partially melt and detach themselves and crash down. This happens principally on the northeast and northwest sides. But the rockslides, like rock avalanches, are worse. Volcanic "bombs," rocks and solidified lava frozen near the crater, roll down the mountain. Some of them are as big as trucks and with a velocity of 80 to 120 mph. Sometimes a rockslide can be started by the jumping of wild goats frightened by climbers. Or a shouted command, an echo, or a shot from a rifle. It is just like the snow avalanches on the Swiss Alps except that here it is thousands and thousands of rocks.

Is weather a danger?

Severe rainstorms and snowstorms can catch you unsuspectedly on the mountain. The worst parts of a storm are the bolts of lightning, which have struck and immobilized climbers.

Doesn't this happen on other mountains as well?

Yes, but not like on Ararat. This is a lone and very high mountain so it is like a gigantic lightning rod. The upper slopes are usually covered with clouds full of static electricity. And climbers carry a lot of metal equipment, picks, crampons, pitons, et cetera. The metal pins on mountaineers' hats, which we use for trading with other climbers, can attract a lightning bolt. The rocks you might try to hide behind are also dangerous. If you are looking for shelter, try to find lava rock—the sharp granite rocks attract lightning.

When you are in the clouds do you lose your way?

No, you stop. If you continue you could step over the side of a gorge or break through the partially melted ice crust over a crevasse going deep down into a glacier. I think that is what happened to two girl climbers who disappeared on the mountain this year [1985]. Remember, you can't know where these holes are. The mountain itself is a volcano and is still "hot." The fog seems to start when hot puffs of gas come from vents in the mountain. When you pitch your tent at a camp after a while you can notice that the earth is giving off heat. In 1965 we had an earthquake here. Just as people were going into the mosque at the time of prayer they suddenly heard a deep and powerful roaring sound that came from inside the earth. After that the earth shook.

I seem to remember hearing that the animal life on Ararat dangerous to climbers could be roughly divided into zones: the lowest zone for poisonous vipers, then the zone for wolves, and finally the zone for bears. Do you agree?

Yes. And don't forget the scorpions when you make camp at the lower levels. They are apt to get under your blanket, sometimes dozens of them, attracted by the heat. A bite or several bites can kill you if you have a bad heart. As for the other kinds of "wild life," the wolves that normally hunt the grazing sheep will attack men if they are hungry enough, and the bears are dangerous if they think you are threatening them. On one climb I started to go for shelter into one of the caves on the mountain but found a mother bear and two cubs already in possession of it. I looked for another cave.

Are there bandits or terrorists on the mountain?

I never saw any. There have been a number of reports published in the newspapers about them during the summer of 1985. But Turkish Army commando units swept the mountain from the top down in August and you can be sure there are no bandits there now.

What Turkish expressions are the most useful for travelers on the mountain?

Here are a few. Some of them could be very important.

Hello!   *Merhaba!*
Please hold your dogs.   *Lütfen köpeği tutun.*
                                (ü = ew, ö = er)

I am lost.	*Kayboldum.*
Please, I need help.	*Lütfen, yardım edin.*
	(ı = a short "uh")
There has been an accident.	*Kaza oldu.*
Where is your camp?	*Çadirlar nerede?*
	(Ç = ch)

(The thing you want comes first in the word order.)

I want food.	*Yiğecek istiyorum. (ğ prolongs the preceding vowel)*
I want water.	*Su istiyorum.*
I want a horse.	*At istiyorum.*
I want a guide.	*Rehber istiyorum.*
How much?	*Ne kadar uzak?*
	(Ne = nay)
How far?	*Ne kadar?*

(The place you are looking for comes first.)

Where is _____?	_____
	nerede?
This way.	*Bu taraftan.*
East	*Doğu*
West	*Batı*
North	*Kuzey*
South	*Güney*
Danger	*Dikkat*
Thank you!	*Sağ ol!*
Goodbye! (To someone leaving)	*Allaha ısmarladık!*
Goodbye! (To someone staying)	*Güle, güle!*
Good! Beautiful!	*Güzel!*

Dr. Arslan, you have had extensive experience as a guide on Mount Ararat and you are an authority on history and folklore. Is the Ark on Ararat?

I believe enough people have seen it within the last fifty or sixty years to establish the truth of the legend. It will probably be found right where it is supposed to be—between 14,000 and 15,000 feet up, following the right-hand side of Ahora Gorge right up to the front of the Parrot Glacier. There is a huge flat plateau there, as big as a football field, a hundred yards deep in ice. This is where, during melting periods, the Ark has been seen and pieces of it have been taken away, and this is where the remains of the Ark will be found.

Nevertheless, although there exists a general belief that the Ark is frozen under the glacier within an ice field over the Ahora Gorge, any expedition formed to dig down to it or remove it would run into several disadvantages. In the first place, Ahora Gorge faces the Russian frontier where military observers are quick to question any noticeable activity on the Turkish side and where, if accomplished by Americans (and news travels fast over the mountain), an official protest would be sure to follow. A search for the Ark in the area where many investigators believe the remnants of the great ship to lie would have to be done quickly and during the summer heat.

But if the Ark has been reported as located at a certain place, why have not exploratory parties followed up the find? The answer to this is furnished by the explicit accounts from ancient times, which took thousands of years to be verified as true. To this category belong the cities of Troy, reputed to be contained in a certain great mound which, when finally excavated, did effectively reveal them; the metropoli of ancient Mesopotamia, covered by mounds and extending *under* the desert, which were rediscovered only by reports from Arab tribes that the giant mounds were a good place to find bricks; and the complete cities of Herculaneum and Pompeii, buried and forgotten for 1500 years and thought to be legends, with most of Herculaneum (the larger) still unexcavated since an Italian town, Resina, has been built *over* the earth covering the ruins. To these examples should be added the Great Sphinx of Giza, whose front paws were suspected to exist and to contain a stone altar, but for almost 2000 years no one took the trouble to dig between the paws to see whether this was true. (It was.)

In other words, all that is needed is a well-organized expedition, equipped with permits, digging implements, and subsurface radar, to test for the presence, and perhaps to find, the Ark on Ararat.

Experiences undergone by expeditions or individuals on Ararat underscore the above list of dangers and suggest a few more. John Morris, the son of Henry M. Morris (Ark researcher and prominent in the Creationist movement), organized an expedition to Mount Ararat in 1972. John Morris subsequently published his own book *(Adventure on Ararat)* in which he describes in vivid terms his encounter with bolt lightning at an elevation of about 13,000 feet. He observed that the lightning seemed to be collecting in certain spots, accompanied by tremendous explosions of thunder.

> Static electricity was evident everywhere. Our ice axes and crampons were singing, our hair was standing on end, even J.B.'s beard and my moustache were sticking straight out. . . .

*   *   *

Despite the storm Morris and two others of his party continued upward and at one point sat under a large rock to rest. Suddenly the rock was repeatedly struck by lightning, knocking Morris and another climber down the slope and "freezing" Bultema (see J.B. above) to the rock with arms and legs extended "out into the air." While stuck to the rock he could feel the electricity "surging through his body" almost completely paralyzing his movements. When he finally was able to force one foot to the ground he unintentionally completed the electrical current causing the force to catapult him down the slope where the others had fallen. Morris, who had lost consciousness from the electric shock, now regained it but still could not move. He saw the third member of the group covered with blood from the sharp rocks. He seemed to be unaware of what had happened and asked, "Why don't we go sit under that big rock and get out of this snow?"—indicating the same rock that had transmitted the lightning shock. Gradually they were able to recover their mobility, probably due to their conditioning as well as psychological force from prayer, and continue painfully back down the mountain.

The 1965 disappearance of a young British mountaineer, Christopher Tease, is especially notable as it serves as a warning not to go climbing alone. Tease, a Balliol student, modestly supported by research grants from Oxford and Balliol College, arrived in Doğubayazit equipped with iron rations which he planned personally to carry up the mountain but with little else. He planned, with extraordinary optimism, to climb to the top of Ararat by August 26 and there, on the summit, to celebrate his birthday. When he did not arrive back in London as he had planned by September

14 his family began making inquiries through the British Embassy in Ankara, which instituted a search involving the Turkish Third Army, the jandarma (the local gendarmerie), and the border police. An official British party, carried by Land-Rover, investigated Tease's disappearance in Agri and Doğubayazit, frequently showing photographs of Tease to local inhabitants to see if anyone recognized him. Two guides who said they had met him at a tea shop in Doğubayazit and were able to speak with him through a student of English from Ağri, reported that they had offered to guide him but he refused their offer since he wished to climb the mountain alone. He was last seen leaving Doğubayazit on foot on his way to climb the mountain, carrying his own pack, with no guide, packhorse or donkey, or even an ice ax.

Despite a liberal reward offered by his parents for information the only report from the British investigative party was that a Kurdish camp on the mountain had been visited by Tease and that the Kurds had offered him a horse. It was later found that the horse had bolted, scattering what equipment he had. It was thought that Tease might have decided to go back to Doğubayazit and disappeared on his return trip.

A subsequent expedition organized by Tease's parents through the Oxford University Explorers Club was equally unsuccessful and concluded that the remains of Tease might be concealed in a crevasse or on a boulder slope. A curious incident occurred while the expedition was in camp. A shepherd approached the camp and asked for the correct time so that he could set his watch, a gold-plated wristwatch with silver expanding bracelet, something of a rarity among shepherds. According to his parents, later questioned, Tease had been wearing a watch of this description when he left on his trip to climb the mountain.

Colonel James Irwin, the astronaut who walked on the moon, founded an organization in 1972 appropriately named High Flight, an international church foundation dedicated in part to the finding of the Ark on Mount Ararat. On his 1982 expedition Colonel Irwin, after reaching the summit, separated from his climbing party for the purpose of returning to base camp to plan the descent. In his book *More Than an Ark on Ararat* he vividly describes what happened to him on the way down.

While taking a short cut across a snowfield at approximately 12,500 feet altitude, he sat down to put on his crampons and suddenly lost consciousness, evidently struck on the head by a rock bouncing down the mountain. He regained consciousness to find himself at the bottom of the snowfield in a pile of sharp rocks bleeding from many cuts and suffering sprains, a possible concussion, and five broken teeth. As night came with its intense cold he was able with difficulty to get into his sleeping bag, but when he fell asleep it would slide further down the mountain and, despite his condition, he would have to pull it back up to the cover of a protective rock. After passing a night of suffering the extreme cold and covered with blood from his numerous cuts, he was contacted by a rescue party and taken by ambulance and helicopter to a hospital in Erzurum.

The fall has not discouraged him: he has taken further expeditions up Ararat in each succeeding year. In his words: "The Ark will be sought year after year. It's a mystery that will live on until it's rediscovered."

Irwin attributes his 1982 escape and return to health to his faith and deep religious commitment. Referring to his own lunar experience he makes a moving comment—"God walking on the earth is more important than man walking on the moon."

During the years 1954 to 1969 John Libi, a resolute searcher for the Ark, made a total of eight research expeditions up Ararat, the last one when he was seventy-three years old. Libi, of Bulgarian origin and of strong religious belief, was convinced that he knew where to find the Ark as he had seen its location in a dream. His climbs on the mountain were not uneventful. He was chased by bears, one of which, he reported, threw stones at him, and was menaced by mountain lions. He was injured when he fell thirty feet onto a rock ledge, was pelted by icy hail as big as tennis balls. He was buried in snow up to his neck and developed pneumonia. On one extensive expedition sudden torrents of rain washed his supplies and equipment down the mountain. A member of his group disappeared over a cliff when the footing at the edge, loosened by an earthquake, suddenly collapsed. An Austrian doctor joined his group during a climb, left camp for a walk, and was never seen again. In his final trip John Libi reached the place where he had dreamed the Ark was situated, but it was not there.

In August 1936 a New Zealand archaeologist (also a British agent), J. Hardwick Knight, approached Ararat from the southeast, crossing the river at the Turkish border south of Sadarak. His crossing was made in some haste in order, in his own words, "to escape from embarrassing followers," who had been pursuing him in Persia (Iran).

Having crossed the Turkish frontier, he intended to circle the slopes of Ararat until he could get to Echmiadzin. But when he approached a camp on the mountain he was suddenly taken prisoner by horsemen who then gave him a mount. The horsemen took him northward to their apparent headquarters and kept him there two days alone in a cellar. Since no horseman would speak to him or allow him to speak he could not tell who they were or why they were keeping him prisoner. At the end of the second day they took him away from headquarters and freed him, on foot, on the mountain. Since the area was covered by fog he could not form an idea of where he was but he proceeded westward, hoping to reach the northern face. As he traveled he encountered explosive electric storms and winds he thought to be up to 100 miles per hour in force. In shock, half asleep, and proceeding by instinct, he eventually passed by a series of timbers protruding from the snow near the rim of Ahora Gorge. His first thought was that they were the remains of artillery carriages or even part of a large barn, although this latter possibility was unlikely at such a height, especially as there are no trees or record of trees on the upper slopes. He did break off a piece of the apparent wood which was soggy and disintegrating and which he lost.

Finally he arrived at Beri. Only later did the idea strike him that he might have passed the Ark. And from then on he regretted that circumstances had not permitted more detailed examination of the timbers he had passed in such haste. He thought more and more about the Ark and in 1967 he returned to Ararat as part of an expedition to investigate the area where he remembered seeing the series of beams. He was unsuccessful: the beams were either deep under snow or had slipped further down the mountain, perhaps into the Ahora Gorge.

Mount Ararat is located within a military zone and

has frequently been closed to climbers for reasons of security. A period of "off limits" was lifted in 1982. This applied, however, only to the southwest side since the northeast side is uncomfortably close to the USSR and the southeast side to the border of Iran.

In 1984 a full-page illustrated article encouraging travel on Mount Ararat appeared in the travel section of *The New York Times* (Sunday, February 19). It gave going rates for transportation to and hotels in Doğubayazit, recommending one for the view and another for the food, as well as giving particulars about how to get there and the in season for mountain climbing. The writer even specified the man to contact in Doğubayazit, Ahmet Aga, giving his telephone number and reporting that he had "bought the title to the southwest slopes of Mount Ararat ten years ago for about $22,000 and that he would not sell it for $4,000,000 today." (This latter statement is probably a mistranslation as no one is permitted to own any part of the mountain. Ahmet Aga simply rents a property from the Turkish government.) According to the Aga (*Aga* is a term of respect) he had said that he *knew* the whole mountain, not that he owned it.

Among expeditions organized after the 1982 ban on climbing there were several conducted by Colonel Irwin and, in 1985, at least four foreign expeditions attempted ascents of the mountain during July and early August. The climbing groups were from Japan, Germany, France, and the USA, with the last three groups on the mountain at practically the same time. The American group, a religious one, was the most Ark-oriented although it is certain that the other groups would examine any wood found on the treeless mountain with considerable interest.

All four groups were captured at night while in their various camps by members of local dissident groups infesting the mountain. The Japanese climbers were the first victims; seized, briefly held and sent down the mountain after being divested of their cameras and special equipment. The American group, from the Probe Ministries Foundation under the combined leadership of Bill Crouse of Dallas, Texas, and John McIntosh, of Crestline, California, had learned about the Japanese incident but, having received permission and hearing that the mountain was officially reopened, made the climb anyway. A Turkish commando unit accompanied them during the first 7000-foot climb and then returned. Other climbers in this group included Jay Bitzer, from Dallas, the expedition photographer; Greg Cromatie, also from Dallas; Wayne Mitchell, of Bound Brook, New Jersey; and Gary Meoski, of Toledo—all capable mountaineers.

On the third day, having reached the 13,500-foot level at the snow line, the Probe group made camp prior to the final push. They were awakened at midnight by shouting. When co-leader Crouse opened his tent flap to see what was happening he stared at the muzzle of a Soviet AK-47, held by a stranger and aimed at his face. The intruders, who seemed to number about eight, confiscated the cold-weather gear necessary for attaining the summit, started a fire with what was burnable, then forced their captives to move quickly down the mountain until they arrived at the 10,800-foot level where the German group had already been intercepted, held, and then chased down the mountain.

Jay Bitzer remembers that the terrorists confiscated all cameras and packed extra gear into rucksacks, forcing the captives to travel down the mountain in the extreme cold without wearing their cold-weather gear. Whenever they hesitated they were urged on by the terrorists and their excitedly held AK-47s. The captors seemed to be in communication with other individuals or bands on the mountain. Bitzer has stated: "They treated each group differently. The French team had to lie on the ground for half an hour." John McIntosh later learned that some of the non-American team members received a more definite discouragement from making future attempts on Ararat. They had their hands tied in back of them, they had been dragged and struck, and finally had to make their way down the mountain at night clad only in their winter underwear. McIntosh thinks that the American team members were treated better perhaps because they had established friendly relationships with the Kurdish horsemen who acted as a buffer between the "kidnappers" and their captives.

McIntosh, a young and agile Californian, has already participated in several climbs up Mount Ararat. He is a convinced believer in the presence of the Ark on some part of the mountain, perhaps hidden under the snow and ice of the glaciers. He has a good eye for detail and remembers a series of incidents in the capture:

> The people who raided our high camp tore down our tents, took what equipment they thought they would need, then they poured our cooking gas on the equipment they didn't want and set it afire. They kept us around the fire and held us there while part of them burned and looted the French camp below us. Then they took us past the French camp to the German camp, what we called the "green camp," past the grassline. There were

more terrorists there; for a moment I thought
that we seemed about to participate in a town
meeting. They had made a number of comments
to us from the time when we were first captured,
most of which we didn't understand but some of
which was clear; that Carter was OK but that
Reagan was definitely "no good" and that (by
gesture) we had offended them by climbing their
mountain. We didn't argue with them since we
didn't know their language and anyway didn't
think it would be a good idea.

Suddenly they started pushing us around and
pointing their guns at us, indicating that we
should stand in a straight line. We didn't know
what was going to happen but, when I saw them
bring their guns to shoulder level and stiffen their
arms as they aimed the guns at us I thought "This
is it!" Jay Bitzer later told me his reaction was, "I
wondered what the hot lead entering one's body
would feel like."

Then, when we were lined up to their satisfaction,
several lowered their guns and produced cameras
and started taking flash pictures of us. After this
their leader, who Bill Crouse said looked just like
Joe Stalin, pointed down the mountain toward
Doğubayazit and said, "Go quick—back to
America!" I don't even remember whether he said
it in English or Turkish, but we certainly got the
meaning. He said something after that which I
think meant, "Don't ever come back on our
mountain!"

*   *   *

Our guides, who had been standing around and occasionally making covert gestures of reassurance to us, shepherded us back down the mountain—the fastest I have ever descended a mountain. The first thing we did on reaching Doğubayazit was to drink a lot of Pepsi, even though it was warm. We were dehydrated.

McIntosh, undaunted by the experience, climbed the mountain again several weeks later with Colonel Irwin's 1985 expedition. The dissident tribesmen had been swept off the mountain by Turkish commandos. Turkish troops also accompanied the new expedition. The summit was reached but the party was forbidden to search the ice fields between the two summit peaks, and returned to base.

Examples of the dangers of oversights in planning and the frustrations of waiting for permission to climb the mountain are furnished in the 1949 expedition of Dr. Aaron Smith, a retired missionary from North Carolina, who headed the first important expedition after World War II up Mount Ararat to search for the Ark. His climbing party of Americans along with Turkish soldiers and guides included Walter Wood, an engineer from Sea Cliff, Long Island, as well as Wendell Org, a physicist at the Oak Ridge Atomic Energy Plant. Org's participation, an example of interest on the part of the science of the future in the legends of the distant past, was to be repeated thirty-six years later, in 1985, by the presence of Los Alamos scientists Drs. John Baumgardner and Mahlon Wilson at the investigation of the buried ark near Mahşer (now called Uzengili) at the 7000-foot altitude.

The crisis in Dr. Smith's expedition came from lack

of water—on a mountain of ice—but at a temperature that makes melting the ice almost impossible. Halfway up the mountain it was found that most of the water had spilled from the cans carried by the pack animals. It was nevertheless decided to push on and to try another possible source of water a day's distance away. But when the party got there there was none. Assiduous searching further on finally located stagnant water in a mountain crevice. The thirsty group scooped it out and drank it while trying to avoid the poisonous snakes and a multitude of insects around it and microbes within it. Fortified by the doubtful water supply the expedition continued, penetrating and examining a number of caverns and crevasses on both sides of the mountain without finding the Ark within the time period allowed them. When their permit expired the snow was already starting to fall on Mount Ararat, precluding any investigation for another year.

Walter Wood was interviewed by the author in Glen Cove, New York.

Question: What did you think at that time [1949] about the dangers of climbing Mount Ararat?

We were the first foreign expedition since before the war. Some of the Turkish press people said we wouldn't get out alive. When we arrived in Istanbul we went to the Turkish police for a permit to search for the Ark on Ararat. The police officer replied (as translated) something like, "Why don't you go to your hotel and get some sleep—you will feel better in the morning," and added, "We have a lot of nice places in Turkey. Why don't you go to one of those?"

Did you go to the American Embassy or Consulate for help?

We got to the consul general. He didn't do much. He wouldn't even hold our money or valuables. I asked: "What do we pay you for?" to which he answered: "You'll see if you get put in jail!" I said: "You mean I'll have to wait until then?"

So we gave up on the Consulate and concentrated on the Turks. They told us to work through the Department of Antiquities, which we did. When we finally got permission to climb the mountain and went to Bayazit they provided guards for us to protect us from Gypsies and smugglers on Ararat. I think the greatest thing that we did was to prove to the Turks that we weren't phonies. I told them: If we are successful you will have the greatest tourist attraction in the world.

Which part of the mountain did you explore?

We were about a month in the area in different parts of the mountain. We even drove around to the Russian side, almost up to the Russian pillboxes and the bridge hanging down at Igdir. (At about this time Russian radio broadcasts continually referred to "American spies wandering in the Ararat area with the pretext of looking for Noah's Ark.")

Wood said he doubted that after four thousand years of volcanic eruptions, storms, and earthquakes the Ark would remain in recognizable form. But shortly after his group came down from the mountain they were approached by native guides who offered to look for the Ark on their own on what might be called a

"contingency" basis—$5000 if they found it or its re-
mains. They went up the mountain, according to Wood,
at times "skipping like mountain goats across broken
rock, and some of them were very old too." When they
came back they said, "No. We are sorry. We thought we
could find it, but this time we didn't. *Inshallah!*"

Egerton Sykes, an English explorer, author, and
researcher of prehistory, veteran of both World Wars,
and frequent traveler in the Middle East, had also
served as under secretary of the British Embassy in Poland. His experience when he tried to get permission
for his own expedition on Ararat is an example of the
disadvantage and possible danger for an individual having close connections with a foreign government.

Sykes had studied the Ararat region's surround-
ings for a number of years and had compiled and published considerable material on Noah's Ark through his
publishing firm, Markham House Press, Brighton, England. He had interested several explorers and mountaineers in his own expedition, which he wished to take
to Ararat in 1949. Because of extensive experience in
Eastern Europe and the Middle East, as well as his fluency in languages and familiarity with past explorations
and legends of the Great Flood, he seemed to be an
extremely well qualified researcher to investigate the
Ark.

Perhaps too qualified. For while he was waiting for
official permission a teletype news report was released
to the German press service indicating the concern of
the Soviet government about Sykes' alleged intelligence
activities. He feared the article presaged denial of his
request. He was correct in his assumption. After the
article appeared he was informed that his permit was
denied. In his words he was "severely attacked in both

Pravda and on Moscow Radio for daring to associate myself with what was a most innocent archaeological visit—which was a great pity!"

There was considerable comment quoted in the world press about this matter by both *Pravda* and Sykes. Among *Pravda*'s editorial comments: "It is easy enough when looking at a map to understand the Biblical amusement of these Anglo-American imperialists. . . . Mount Ararat is situated in Turkey and Persia but overlooks Soviet Armenia. The Sykes expedition is financed to spy out our territory." To this Sykes replied that if there were enough ice on Mount Ararat to preserve the Ark for thousands of years it would be too cold for him to sit there "peering through a telescope at an expanse of Russian desert." The *Calcutta Statesman* warned Sykes editorially that in the event he climbed up Ararat he should be careful which side he came down on since if he came down on the wrong side the Russian secret police who would be waiting for him would probably be unconvinced about his archaeological status even if he had relics of the Ark as ". . . they believe, alas, more in spies than in the Bible."

6

Reported Encounters With the Ark

There exist a number of statements from persons who claim to have seen the Ark from close up, touched it, or even taken away pieces of it and exhibited them. These reports are from relatively modern times and have been widely circulated in the international press and have been commented on in a number of books. It is notable, however, that even in modern times no photographs definitely showing the Ark have been available to the public from the time of the two Russian expeditions during the Tsarist regime to the mountain climbers and Ark-searching expeditions, mainly religiously motivated, from the United States. Such photographs as have been reportedly taken have either been lost or considered inconclusive, and the photographs taken from space up to now show too small an object to permit definite examination or anything more than an approximate measurement.

Lack of definite proof of the Ark's existence has

had little effect on the millions who believe in its actuality, whether Christians, Moslems, or Jews in different parts of the world or a number of people living close to Ararat in Turkey, Iran, or in the Armenian SSR.

Tom McNellis, an American business representative living in Germany, visited the northeastern and northwestern lower slopes of Mount Ararat in the summer of 1985 and confirmed a general belief among local inhabitants in a conversation with the author in Doğubayazit. McNellis found that his fluency in German was a breakthrough in communicating with the local inhabitants; especially with older Turkish officers having had German military training with memories and traditions of World War II, as well as with younger men who had found employment in Germany and returned. McNellis observed that many people in villages on the northern slopes of Mount Ararat believed that the Ark could be fairly easily located—"You just follow the left side of the Ahora Gorge and when you reach the top of the gorge turn left. Soon you will find the Ark. . . ."

The Ark is not visible from the lower levels, he was told, principally because the glacier or the snow on the glacier has covered it since it came down from the upper heights of the mountain thousands of years ago.

It has long been suggested that the key to sighting or visiting the Ark may consist of certain cycles of warm weather which cause melting around the Ark or a *shift* in the surrounding ice which brings the great ship into temporary view. Egerton Sykes, having studied weather cycles pertaining to the Ark for some years, was of the opinion that the shorter cycles were at seven-year intervals with even warmer cycles approximately every twenty years.

An Associated Press article by correspondent Edward Greenwald in November 1948 reported that a Turkish farmer named Reşit (pronounced *Reshit*) had apparently encountered a ship on the mountain during one of these warm-weather periods. It is especially pertinent since Reşit had been in the area a number of times and had not seen anything of the sort on his previous trips. The person who made the report to Greenwald was not Reşit but a landowner of the district, Shukru Asena, who visited the AP bureau in Istanbul to report the incident.

Greenwald's report indicated that Reşit, at an altitude of about 11,000 to 12,000 feet, had discovered what seemed to be the prow of a ship protruding over the edge of a canyon into which melting ice and snow had been falling. Reşit said that the prow was "about the size of a house." The rest of the "ship" was covered, running back into the ice and snow. (Note: This description, perhaps a seasonal phenomenon, is almost the same as the reports by Lieutenant Schwinghammer and other pilots of the 428th Tactical Squadron already described.) The report continued:

> Reşit climbed down to it and with his dagger tried to break off a piece of the prow. It was so hard it would not break. It was blackened with age. Reşit insisted it was not a simple rock formation. "I can recognize a ship when I see one," he said. "This is a ship!" (This is almost the exact statement made by David Fasold thirty-eight years later. Fasold, however, with long underwater diving and salvage experience, is equally or even more qualified to make such an observation.)

*   *   *

Alerted by Reşit's report, villagers climbed up the northern slope of the mountain and inspected the strange boatlike object, concurring that it effectively was part of a large ship. This news item was picked up by papers all over the world as have been other reports of reputed discoveries of the Ark on Mount Ararat. Such reports have given considerable impetus to other expeditions such as that of Dr. Aaron Smith, whose vicissitudes were described in the previous chapter, and a number of other expeditions as well. But although Reşit has been much sought he has not been found on Ararat.

Tim LaHaye and John Morris, authors of a definitive work on Ark research, *The Ark on Ararat,* suggest that Reşit's evidently voluntary disappearance from the scene was because he, being a Turk and a Moslem, might have been unwilling to participate in a search undertaken by a strongly religious foreign Christian group and thought it might be more advisable to fade back into anonymity.

Probably the best-known and certainly the most publicized in the press among the various personal encounters with the Ark has been that of Fernand Navarra, a French industrialist from Bordeaux and the author of *J'ai trouvé l'arche de Noé.* His career and reported discovery are reminescent of those of Heinrich Schliemann, a successful German businessman of the last century who dreamed from the age of seven of discovering Troy, at that time still considered a legend. After Schliemann had made his fortune in his fur business in Germany he traveled to Turkey, employed diggers, and proved the legend to be true by digging into a great hill and finding a succession of superimposed cities including, at one level, the real Troy of the Trojan War.

Navarra felt an identical fascination for the legend of the Ark from the time the story was first told to him at the age of four after he had been fished out of a pond into which he had fallen. His mother told him the story of the Ark to calm him. He never forgot it, and decided that someday he would look for it.

He was later fortified in his determination to find it one day by an incident which occurred while he was serving with the French Army in Syria prior to World War II. When he was off duty he liked to take long climbs on hills and mountains around Damascus and, in the course of one of his hikes, he started to climb Mount Hebron with an Armenian friend named Alim. Although Alim dropped out before reaching the top, Navarra climbed up to the 11,000-foot summit and stayed there for several hours. Alim, waiting for him below, thought Navarra was lost or dead and was so happy to see him alive that he began to tell him of his memories of Mount Ararat and how his grandfather had told him that the Ark was still accessible to be viewed by climbers. Alim urged Navarra to climb Ararat for him and to find the Ark for the world. This encouragement was an inspiration to Navarra and through the years he amassed a great deal of information about the Ark as well as a considerable amount of money through the operation of his company (demolitions) which would later afford him ample funds for his quest.

Navarra's first expedition (1952) was unsuccessful in proving the existence of the Ark to the world but the chance sighting of a huge dark object resembling a ship *underneath* the ice of a glacier to him was conclusive proof of its existence. It would also furnish him with a landmark (if one can be established on a moving glacier) for subsequent expeditions.

Having applied in Ankara, and obtaining after a

certain period of waiting, permission to climb Mount
Ararat, Navarra; the explorer and alpinist Baron Jean
de Riquier; Alaaddin Seker, a Turkish filmmaker and
mountain climber; and three others traveled to Doğubayazit. From there the party, accompanied from time
to time by members of the local police, herdsmen, and
horsemen when feasible, made a number of exploratory
climbs on the eastern and northeastern sides of the
mountain, sometimes quite close to the Russian border,
at the present time definitely off limits. The party experienced the usual discomforts, such as snowslides, bliz-
zards, electrical storms, infestations of mosquitoes,
smashed and ripped supplies from the mule train, but
finally reached the top of Ararat in August 1962.

A second series of climbs up the Ahora trail toward
Küp Lake revealed that what many considered a possible Ark on the mountain was simply a large rock spur, a
feature which the monks from Echmiadzin were accus-
tomed to show to travelers through the monastery telescope as what they believed to be a firsthand view of the
Ark. After Küp Lake was passed, the party proceeded
upward, leaving some members at 13,500 feet altitude.
Navarra and de Riquier proceeded to 15,000 feet and,
crossing an arm of the glacier, mounting a dome and
looking down, saw below under the ice of a glacier a
long dark mass resembling the outline of a ship's hull.
(The sun was at an angle of 45°, lessening light reflection and tending to make the ice more transparent.)
Other beamlike shapes under the ice continued to outline the oblong shape. The two explorers paced it off by
walking on top of the glacier and estimated a length of
380 to 400 feet. In his book *J'ai trouvé l'arche de Noé*
Navarra describes his feelings on viewing the phenomenon:

"At that altitude, in that desert of ice, what could it

be? The ruins of a building, church, refuge or house, never mentioned in any account, any tradition, never seen by any of those who came to this place?" Navarra wondered if the beams might be the wreckage of a plane that had crashed into the upper levels of the mountain but, as he mentions in his book, great beams were never used in the construction of aircraft. He wrote: "I had to accept the evidence, these remains were those of the Ark . . . they could not be anything else." He concluded that it was possible that he was looking through the translucent ice at beams from the keel or hull of the Ark and surmised that the upper structure had been separated through the years from the lower hull.

Navarra noted that the buried outline seemed to be connected by thick straight lines which resembled large beams, such as would have been used in the construction of a great ship. But, as the large and small rocks which were falling intermittently from above made further examination too dangerous and time consuming to accomplish at that moment, Navarra took a reading of his position as accurately as possible so that he could return at a later time for a more complete investigation of the intriguing shadow under the ice.

A return trip the following year was no more productive. Navarra, accompanied by Alaaddin Seker, reached the site but became affected by dizziness and had to go back down the mountain. Nevertheless Navarra was able to take pictures of the object through the ice, photographs which, understandably, were not entirely convincing.

Back in France he followed an intensive training program in mountain climbing and kept in practice by climbing a number of mountains in the Alps and Pyrenees.

In 1955 he returned to Turkey, ostensibly as a

tourist, accompanied by his wife and three sons. The object of the trip was solely to climb Ararat and to bring back some conclusive proof of having seen or touched the Ark. The year seemed propitious—it was the geodesic year of 1955, when the glaciers would be at their greatest thaw point in decades. (It was in this year that an international expedition exploring in Antarctica made the unexpected discovery that Antarctica was composed of two, not one land mass, information previously not known in modern times although indicated on ancient seafaring maps drawn thousands of years before Antarctica was officially discovered and evidently at an epoch before it was covered by ice.)

Possibly in order to avoid delays or refusal in obtaining a permit to climb Ararat, Navarra, accompanied by his family, approached his target in an indirect and leisurely manner designed to allay suspicions of what his real purpose might be. (A prospective climber would scarcely take his wife and children up the dangerous mountain, and travel in Eastern Turkey by foreigners was forbidden at this time.)

They entered Turkey through Syria and Navarra took due note that the Turkish consul informed him that the Ararat area and parts of Eastern Turkey were prohibited to foreign tourists. Nevertheless Navarra crossed the border and proceeded by car to Lake Van in the prohibited section, simply asking their way as they went. Following a zigzag path they approached Erzurum, a large town on the way to Ararat. When stopped Navarra showed the authorities his Iranian visa and, since Erzurum is on the way to Iran, his explanation was accepted. They obtained quarters at a hotel in Karakosi at some distance from Doğubayazit, the large town closest to Ararat and, having established a base there, the entire family drove to Doğubayazit, passing by the police station stop point with a cordial wave (but without stopping) and drove part of the way up the western slope of Ararat. There the party stopped and Navarra and his youngest son, Rafaël, aged eleven, started up the mountain alone, carrying their provisions. They had reached their first goal without a permit, a tactic scarcely to be recommended then and one especially to be avoided in subsequent years.

This father and son team apparently succeeded in finding "pieces of the Ark" and, an almost equally difficult feat, bringing one piece down the mountain and out of Turkey. What happened to them during their four days and nights on the mountain, enduring a sudden storm and blizzard, constant climbing from crest and down crevasses, Navarra being hit by an avalanche rock, snowed within an ice cave for thirteen hours and trying to keep from being frozen, are a reminder of the meaning of Ağri Dağh (the Mountain of Pain) and also a tribute to the conditioning and perseverance of the two searchers. When the storm stopped and the sky cleared, Navarra found that they were at the mound on the edge of the glacier under which he thought he had seen the Ark on a previous trip. The ice mass now had developed breaks and crevasses, some of which went down twenty-five to thirty or more feet to where water was flowing through the bottom part of the glacier, an indication that considerable melting was taking place. To his delight Navarra saw lines resembling the "beams" he had previously photographed. But then, as he suddenly realized that the moraine dust had made patterns under the ice, it occurred to him that he had photographed volcanic dust patterns suggesting a nonexistent Ark.

His son Rafaël rescued him from his dilemma by

asking him why he didn't cut into one of the patterns. He took this advice and let himself down on a rope ladder into the crevasse and found that under the dust patterns there were wooden beams, wood that was evenly cut and obviously hand-tooled. He tried to lift a piece out of the melting ice but it appeared to be still attached to something else—in Navarra's opinion, the hull. With considerable difficulty he cut through a beam and hoisted up a five-foot piece of it. Although delighted by this success and convinced that he had found and cut off a sample of the "world's oldest shipwreck" he realized the difficulties he would encounter in getting the artifact off the mountain and out of the country. He cut the piece of the Ark into three sections and distributed them in different packs.

At the foot of Mount Ararat soldiers stopped them and ordered them to empty their backpacks. They were especially interested in the cameras (then forbidden on the mountain) and asked to have their pictures taken, overlooking the remnants of the Ark which, in Navarra's opinion, they thought was firewood. Although the "firewood" had passed inspection, Navarra still had to explain why he was in a prohibited area without authorization. During an interview with the local governor he spoke to him so convincingly of his interest in mountain climbing and in the famous Mount Ararat that the governor not only overlooked the infringement but offered him a permit to climb up the mountain from which he had just climbed down, an offer which Navarra courteously declined.

Before returning to France Navarra and his family visited Egypt where he submitted a piece of the wood to the Cairo Museum, Archaeological Section, for an opinion. He was told that the wood was from 5000 to 6000 years of age and the Egyptian Ministry of Agriculture gave an estimate of 5000 B.C. and added that the blackened beam was made of oak. (It is to be noted that the term "gopherwood," used in Genesis to describe the wood of which the Ark was constructed, has been generally qualified by scientists to mean *white oak*. As there is no white oak within 600 miles of Mount Ararat it is logical to assume that a ship of white oak must have been constructed at a considerable distance from Ararat and was carried there by men or washed up on the mountain by a great wave.) Through the use of carbon-14 tests and other methods later estimates of the wood's age came from the universities of Bordeaux and Madrid (4000 to 5000 years old), the University of California (1250 years old), and a less favorable upgrade from the University of Pennsylvania laboratory (A.D. 560).

It should be remembered that dating of ancient objects made of wood or any other once living organism by the carbon-14 method is only approximate. Carbon does not always decay at a predictable rate and sometimes industrial or fuel residue can make a wooden object, by applying carbonization *in situ,* catalogue as much older than it could possibly be. This has been demonstrated by carbon testing of fallen branches from trees along the *Autobahnen* of Germany which were planted *after* the highways were completed. Present dating techniques are more extensive than they were and include atomic and archaeomagnetic studies, spectroanalysis, potassium-argon testing and thermoluminescence. It would be interesting to examine the Ark fragments—if enough are available after the preceding tests—to determine more exactly how old they really are. For while the examinations of the wood submitted by Navarra attest to a considerable though variable age according to where they were tested, the dates still go back only to a period of recorded world history and not to an age of legend where great catastrophes shook and flooded the earth unless, of course, the deep freeze and covering of the wood inhibited the carbon-14 decay.

Navarra, by this time world-famous, returned to his find several times after 1965. He brought back more wood but at times there remained an air of mystery about where he had found it. Some Ararat explorers and writers about the Ark have suggested that some of the wood he later found was brought from Spain, taken up the mountain and then "discovered" up on the slopes under the ice. It has also been pointed out by the competent Ark archivist and author Violet Cummings (*Has Anyone Really Seen Noah's Ark?*), wife of Eryl Cummings, climber of Mount Ararat and possessor of the most complete files on the search for the Ark, that on some subsequent climbs Navarra seemed to lead exploratory parties to other parts of the mountain, away from the area he had previously described.

Ahmet Ali Arslan acted as a guide on one of Navarra's subsequent climbs, together with Bud Crawford and a French-English interpreter in 1968. Arslan expressed his great admiration for Navarra as a skilled alpinist and explorer and states he is grateful for what Navarra taught him about mountaineering. He describes Navarra as jovial, good-natured, and enthusiastic, as far as Arslan could tell, since Navarra spoke only in French through the interpreter.

The party was on the mountain about two weeks. When they were on the upper slopes near Küp Lake an incident occurred that was never explained. Navarra suddenly walked away from the camp. According to Arslan:

Looking north over Abich I Glacier. The neck between the two summits is the point from where avalanches come down into the Black Glacier. *Ahmet Ali Arslan*

When Ahmet Ali Arslan attempted to use this cave on the Black Glacier as a refuge he found that it was preempted by a bear and her cubs. *Ahmet Ali Arslan*

The entrance to this cave below the Parrot Glacier was revealed by chipping away the covering ice. Ahmet Ali Arslan dropped into the deep cave and took pictures while hanging from a rope. The white light on bottom is a reflection of the sun shining on snow. *Ahmet Ali Arslan*

A sudden fog has overtaken a climbing party on the eastern slope of Mount Ararat. Climbers will have to wait until fog lifts to avoid falling into crevasses or over the edge of a precipice. *Ahmet Ali Arslan*

Horseshoe Valley, northeast of Ahora, filling with sudden fog. *Ahmet Ali Arslan*

Author with mountain-bred horse used for climbing. The horse's adornments and harness are typical of local custom. Background shows the tip of Ararat. There are also wild horses on the mountain which move in herds for mutual protection against wolves and bears. *Ahmet Ali Arslan*

Ice melting on Parrot Glacier. The erratic melting pattern opens up entrances and galleries under the ice where a number of explorers believe the Ark may be found. Water does not reappear in rivers or streams but subsequently is seen as fountains on the Karabulak Plain. *Ahmet Ali Arslan*

Ahora Glacier showing the moraine ice covered by dust and rocks. Streams coming from the melting ice provide the water supply for villages lower on the mountain. *Ahmet Ali Arslan*

Ahmet Ali Arslan negotiates a crevasse with the aid of an ice ax. On one occasion he crashed through the light ice coating and fell thirty feet into the crevasse before getting out with the help of his ice ax, ropes, and two assistants. *Ahmet Ali Arslan*

Sheep on mountain above Ahora Gorge. These regional sheep are raised mainly for export and are shipped to Iran, Iraq, and Syria. *Ahmet Ali Arslan*

Melting ice off Parrot Gorge running into a fissure on the northeast side. Navarra reported in 1965 that the remains of the Ark lie here under the ice, at this point over 150 feet deep. During the customary August melting hundreds of holes form and melting ice runs off into glacial waterfalls. *Ahmet Ali Arslan*

The arrow marks the spot where insurgent bandits attacked the Probe team in 1985. Other higher folds in the mountain, partially covered by ice, show the position where pilots have seen a shiplike object from the air and explorers claim to have seen it exposed or under the ice. © *Jay Bitzer, Probe Ministries, 1985*

Typical danger area on Ahora Gorge where light snow, wind, and fog can cause climbers to fall into crevasses or chasms. *Ahmet Ali Arslan*

Glacier flowing from Mıh Tepe down upper slope of Great Ararat. *Ahmet Ali Arslan*

*　　*　　*

He didn't say where he was going. When he had
been gone for several hours I became worried.
Even a skilled mountaineer like him could have an
accident; could fall over a cliff or down a hole in
the ice and stay there. After some hours he came
back. He did not say where he had been or what
he had been doing. I don't know what he said to
his interpreter. When I asked about it I got no
answer. . . .

Although pieces of wood have been found on the
snow-covered treeless slopes some of them have doubt-
lessly been carried up to be burned as firewood by
climbers. But light pieces of wood in or under the snow
are not comparable to large worked beams suitable for
heavy construction of ships or barges. These beams
have been found at altitudes fairly near the summit by
Kurdish or Turkish mountaineers. These climbers do
not generally make a report about such a find (except in
the case of Reşit who reported finding an entire ship)
since they believe it constitutes only one more corroboration of something about which they are already
aware—the presence of a great ship on Ararat.

Ismaïl Vural, a retired mill owner living in Aralik, a
town on the northeast side of Ararat, has lived in the
area all his life. His age can be calculated by the fact that
he remembers the period of World War I. At that time
he participated not in the war but in a raid designed to
repossess the family flock of sheep which had been
stolen on the mountain by shepherds during the con-
fused times of World War I. His clan, led by his uncle,
surrounded the sheep stealers' village and got the flock
back—with interest. His memory is clear about the long-
ago incident—"We got our revenge. I remember it all."

His recollection is also very clear about an object he found near the top of Ararat in 1939. Ismaïl was interviewed in Turkish by Ahmet Ali Arslan in August 1985 at his home in Aralik.

Question: When and why did you decide to climb Mount Ararat?

It was in 1939. The soldiers came to practice climbing on the mountain. Our people asked if they had climbed to the top and they said they had, but our people didn't believe them. A property owner named Fassan was blown off the mountain by winds and that's why they thought it was impossible to climb. My uncle Mehmet Ali had climbed up with him and told us what happened. They climbed to the upper slopes and then the wind caught Fassan and blew him off the mountain. He fell through the air and kept falling like a wisp of cotton. Although the soldiers said that they had climbed it our people said that the Mountain of Nūh (Noah) could not be climbed and that it would keep its secrets.

Did you think differently?

Yes. I explained to a few friends that they might be wrong because Turkish soldiers would not lie about the results of a mission. I said, "Let's join them and find out if they really went to the top." We tried to join a military group from Kars. We got permission from the local commandant, who first refused because we were not in the army but then he changed his mind.

A lieutenant from Sarikamiş was in charge

aided by a Second Lieutenant Sevket. We climbed to Sardar Bulak and another army group climbed Lesser Ararat. They gave us anoraks and climbing boots although I didn't get the boots. As we went up Ararat I climbed with the officers and we followed the footsteps of the enlisted men who went ahead.

We had almost reached the summit, maybe ten meters away. I was looking for a pencil to write down my name and date on something but I couldn't find one. Then I noticed a long beam sticking out of the snow—about three meters long.

What did it look like?

Both sides were hand-hewn and showed marks of a cutting ax. It was thick and it was square, not round. It was cut with a groove for another piece to fit into it. I looked around for another piece but more pieces must have been under the snow.

Did you think that it might be a piece of Noah's Ark?

Not at the time. I thought, "By Allah! We certainly didn't carry this ourselves as well as carry our equipment. What idiotic *hamal* [heavy-duty porter] would carry this beam all the way to the top by himself?" If Noah's Ark had entered my mind I never would have left it there. I later heard from other climbers that there were other pieces under the ice.

We ate some of our provisions and then we washed our faces, hands, and chests with snow because it was a holy place.

What happened to the beam?

Years later a group of my friends found it. They left it there. Then, many years later, French climbers came and found wood and our newspapers wrote about it. I don't know if it was the same wood.

Why didn't you tell the foreigners about the wood you found?

If they had asked me I would have told them. They didn't ask.

Do people around the mountain believe in the Ark of Nūh, and that perhaps you found a piece of it?

Not only me but all the people in the towns believe it. Our grandfathers and their grandfathers have believed it since ancient times. It is like I have told my son. It is a holy mountain and the Ark of Nūh is near the top and it will stay there because it is the command of Allah. This is the secret of the mountain and the mountain will keep its secret.

A number of past or present dwellers in villages on Mount Ararat have claimed to have seen or even touched the Ark although they have not communicated their experiences to the press, probably for reasons of secrecy, religion, or even personal security. George Hagopian, mentioned in Chapter 3, an Armenian born near Lake Van, once a soldier in the Turkish Army, later a refugee and prisoner in the USSR, and finally an American citizen, did not reveal his own pilgrimage to the Ark until 1970, at a time when reports on expeditions to the Ark were attaining a steadily increasing interest in the world press. It is understandably difficult to assume that a single witness is telling the exact truth about something that he personally saw or experienced more than half a century ago, especially about something as legendary as the Ark. Hagopian's experience, told to a friend, came to the attention of the Search organization and Eryl Cummings, Elfred Lee, and René Noorbergen met with and interviewed Hagopian. He recounted boyhood encounters with the Ark with assurance and convincing sincerity. He repeated and elaborated his story over a series of interviews, answering questions put to him at intervals over a year and a half. He continued to give unequivocal answers in picturesque yet understandable English. He collaborated with Elfred Lee, a photographer and artist as well as a researcher, in helping him make a sketch of what he had seen and vividly remembered.

He was eight years old, Hagopian said, and it was in the year 1908 when his uncle took him up Ararat, past Ahora Gorge, passing the grave of St. Jacob on the way. As the mountain grew more precipitous his uncle carried him on his shoulders until they came to something that looked like a great ship located on a rock ledge over a cliff and partially covered by snow. It had flat openings like windows along the top and a hole in the roof. Hagopian had first thought it was a house made of stone but when his uncle showed him the outline of planks and told him it was made of wood he realized it was the Ark, just like other people had described it to him. His uncle boosted him up from a rock pile to reach the Ark roof telling him not to be afraid, "because it is a holy ship . . ." (and) "the animals and people are not here now. They have all gone away."

Hagopian climbed on the roof and knelt down and kissed the surface of the roof which was flat and easy to stand on.

While they stood alongside the Ark his uncle shot into the side of it but the bullets bounced off as if it were made of stone. He then tried to cut off a piece of the wood with a sharp knife and was equally unsuccessful. On this first visit to the Ark they spent two hours there looking at it and eating some of their provisions. When Hagopian returned to his village eager to tell the other boys about his adventure they replied, rather anti-climactically, "Yes, we saw that Ark too."

Hagopian died in 1972. Since he was unable to read maps with any accuracy he was unable to pinpoint on a map of the mountain where it was that he had seen and climbed on the Ark. He consistently told his inter-rogators that if he could get back to Mount Ararat he

Noah's Ark resting on a ledge on Mount Ararat as drawn by Elfred Lee according to a description given to him by George Hagopian, who claimed that, as a boy, he visited the Ark with his father and climbed on its roof. *Drawing © Elfred Lee*

could lead a party to the Ark. Although his testimony was successfully approved by voice-stress analysis, it is not unusual that reports such as this, from a single person, even if firsthand, have been discredited because of lack of corroboratory evidence from others. But there exists another piece of corroboration connected with Lieutenant (now Captain) Schwinghammer's sighting of a boatlike object on Mount Ararat as observed from an aircraft belonging to the 428th Tactical Observation Squadron (see Chapter 3).

In 1983 Schwinghammer had asked an artist friend to draw, under his direction, a sketch of what he had seen before it became too blurred in his memory. Elfred Lee, on his part, while interrogating Hagopian, had drawn a detailed sketch of the reported ship on the mountain (see page 102), which was done in Hagopian's presence and under his direction. Neither Schwinghammer nor Hagopian knew of the other's existence nor of any sketch made of Hagopian's "Ark."

Captain Schwinghammer had been asked by the author to send a copy of his sketch and, after doing so, Schwinghammer received in the mail almost at the same time and without having requested it the picture of the Lee–Hagopian version. To Schwinghammer's astonishment the two sketches were essentially the same: the Ark was in the same position on the mountain and both pictures showed a rectangular boat or barge on a ledge over a precipice.

When Schwinghammer saw the drawing he said, "That looks just like what I saw. The object had the same angle on the mountain and the position was the same. The only difference is that I did not notice any 'windows' along the top." This is understandable because of the aircraft's speed and altitude and also because the object was partially covered by snow.

Perhaps the most striking aspect of Schwinghammer's sighting was that it was made on the northeast side
of Mount Ararat, where Hagopian, Navarra, and others
claimed to have seen the lost Ark. While Schwinghammer did not specify or even know of Ahora Gorge, his
flight had approached Ararat from the south and had
continued counterclockwise east and northeast about
halfway around the peak when he sighted the "object," a
pattern which would have put him in the vicinity of the
Parrot Glacier over the Ahora Gorge.

In recent years public interest has been rekindled
through a series of articles in religious, exploration, and
scientific magazines (both for and against the Ark's existence although mostly against in scientific publications),
reports in the daily press, lectures by explorers and researchers of the Ark, investigative books and even nov-
els, and recent movies concerning the Ark have had
worldwide distribution.

Even the scientific community, having long considered reports about the reality of the Ark with humor-
ous or scornful skepticism or as a story fit only for
children, has given signs of interest in a possible buried
construction high on Ararat. The present science editor
of *The New York Times,* Walter Sullivan, wrote in a report
dealing with Noah's Ark (February 26, 1970) that the
Arctic Institute of North America "probably the fore-
most polar service on this continent" had decided to
assist an Ararat expedition in removing the ice cover
over a reported "50 tons of hewn beams" at an altitude
of 14,000 feet. The article mentioned Navarra's finding
of the beams but carefully avoided a direct suggestion
that the timbers belonged to the Ark, stating that scientific interest was provoked by the "evidence that some
sort of structure—apparently a large one—existed 1300
years ago near the summit [of Ararat]."

Worldwide publicity about Noah's Ark has attracted each year to Doğubayazit an increasing number of searchers for the Ark, explorers, mountain climbers, members of religious groups, archaeologists, members of the world press, television personnel, and sightseers, all dedicated to varying degrees to finding the Ark, seeing it, or disproving it. They come to Doğubayazit during the last months of summer, at the time of the greatest melting of the glaciers and ice fields—a yearly phenomenon contributing to the prosperity of Doğubayazit and the overcrowding of the few hotels. If the other towns in the vicinity of the mountain were again to be opened to the public it is to be assumed that this would be repeated in Igdir, Aralik, and Ahora.

In the last eighteen years several very ambitious Ark-finding projects were organized but failed to eventuate either due to withholding of mountain-climbing permits, the delicate international situation on Turkey's eastern border, activity of dissidents on the mountain, and often too short periods of climbing because of delays in obtaining permits.

Some of these projects show high determination and imagination. In 1967, before the mountain was put off limits in the '70s, the ARF (Archaeological Research Foundation: Chairman, George Vanderman) presupposed a budget of $1,000,000 for a 1968 expedition to be filmed in cooperation with Cinerama. The expedition was to communicate while on the mountain with walkie-talkies and to use large tractors capable of pulling heavy bedded trailers. As the Cinerama connection did not eventuate, a less extensive expedition was successful in uncovering more wood. Another organization, SEARCH (Scientific Exploration and Archaeological Research), in a preliminary survey in 1970, reported that the Arctic Institute of North America calculated that 900,000 cubic meters of ice and moraine had to be removed from the subject area. Ralph Crawford, president of SEARCH, calculated that $300,000 had already been spent on research and that the cost of removing the moraine that had fallen from the cliff overhanging the object would be over $1,000,000. It was noted that heavy power equipment would be needed and that excavation equipment should be flown in by helicopter.

A plan for locating the Ark and performing excavations through the use of aircraft not only for observation but as a working tool was formulated by a well-known aviator, Louis McCollum. McCollum, owner and operator of McCollum Aviation, a company for the chartering and sales of aircraft and a pilot with great experience with and knowledge of aircraft potentialities, offered to cooperate with SEARCH in an air expedition to look for the Ark and find it even if it were now under the ice and snow in the gorges or under the glaciers of the mountain. He envisaged using a high-flight helicopter as a means of transportation for personnel and equipment to the presumed Ark site, thus avoiding the usual loss of valuable melting time spent in climbing to the snowline. The helicopter itself was to be transported to Turkey in a DC-7 cargo plane.

During a waiting period caused by delays in obtaining permits and other authorizations, McCollum, during a dinner appointment with President Nixon, took the opportunity to inform the then president of his project and to enlist his aid. President Nixon referred him to the State Department which, in turn, advised him to put the project "on hold" pending the arrival of a more secure international political climate in the area than there was in 1970–1971.

McCollum later explained the principal features of his plan as to how the Ark could be found and examined in an interview reported by Dave Balsiger and Charles Sellier in their book *In Search of Noah's Ark* as well as later to the author in telephone conversations regarding participation in a joint exploration project using helicopters. McCollum's plan included the use of a Bell 47G3B-1 supercharged helicopter for the transportation (half a ton per flight) of men and equipment to an initial total of twenty to thirty tons to a campsite on the ice pack. Drilling in the suspect area would be accomplished with core power drills to establish the outline of the ship with later probes to be made between the outlines in a search for frozen animal remains, bones, or food supplies. After these initial probes a special blowtorch would be used to dig a tunnel from the surface down into the Ark, and when the passage was enlarged enough to permit research personnel to work at the bottom a geodesic dome would be placed on top of it, to be followed by more passages and more domes enabling researchers to work in a controlled environment and thus to be protected from falling rocks, snow, and icefalls.

McCollum died before this unusual project could be tested. It is in any case doubtful whether such excavating would be permitted on the mountain especially in view of the frequent Soviet protests about activity near the border of Armenia, an SSR (Soviet Socialist Republic). It is predictable and natural that Russia would object to large-scale excavations on the part of the mountain facing or looking down on Russia. The Soviets, having successfully blocked Egerton Sykes, the British explorer and writer and expert on the area, from participation in an Ararat expedition, now seem to consider American investigative expeditions on Mount Ararat as an activity of the CIA, one of the reasons the northeastern side of the mountain is now forbidden to foreign climbing parties.

Paradoxically, considering the antireligious stance of the Soviet government, Russian investigation of Ararat has played an important role in Ark research. This has been true since Parrot's first successful ascent, then through the reported sightings of the Ark in World War I by military aircraft, engineer, and infantry units, more sightings in World War II, this time by Soviet pilots flying over Mount Ararat who told Allied airmen about it and allegedly showed photographs of the Ark, and also by a Russian commander of a camouflage unit (Major Jasper Maskelyn) who sent a mission over Mount Ararat that allegedly verified the 1916 report from the Russian Imperial Air Force.

Present official Soviet policy is generally opposed to the spread and teaching of religion and emphatically to the authentication of a religious legend that could have such influence in the renewal of religious beliefs. But the general Soviet policy has not affected religion in Armenia. Mount Ararat is clearly visible from Erivan, the capital of the Armenian SSR, and is a constant reminder to Armenians of Noah, the Ark, the Flood, and of Ararat, called Massis in Armenian—"the Mother of the World."

7

The Tides That Swept the World

The story of the Great Flood and the survival of a man, together with his family and animals in an ark or ship (and sometimes other means) has existed in legends and folktales for more than 3000 years and perhaps as far back as 11,000 years—coincidentally the time of the melting of the last glaciers. The race memory of the world's peoples shares close variations of this legend from the ages before history. We do not presently know how long man had existed on the earth in a civilized state (although our calculations go further back with new discoveries from year to year) before a tremendous catastrophe changed the face of the earth, killing most of the earth's inhabitants, animal and human.

The legends that have come down to us over the centuries indicate that this catastrophe was either a worldwide deluge or a combination of floods, fire, and shakings of the earth. It has been suggested that a collision with an asteroid or slipping and melting of the glaciers and ice caps caused the careening of the planet, the shifting of mountain ranges as well as the sinking of land masses into the ocean. This event is frequently rep-

109

resented in the legends of pre-history as having caused the death of *all* people and animals except those on the ark or ship or saved by other means of survival. In most cases the lucky ones had been warned by God or particular deities that the anger of heaven was about to destroy mankind and that they should construct a ship before the deluge that was to come. Then, after the waters receded, the survivors left their ship or shelter and proceeded to repopulate the earth. There are over 600 variations of this legend among the ancient nations and tribes and the story has been told through the millennia in all quarters of the globe. The variations in accounts of the catastrophe, as could be expected, occur principally in regional modifications of the same story, such as the description of the Ark, the reasons for heavenly displeasure, the way chosen individuals were saved, and even the possibility of the doom happening again. The name of the chief protagonist, Noah, is easily recognizable in Hebrew, and in the languages of the Christian and Moslem worlds (in Arabic—*Nūh*).

The story of the Flood, Noah, and the Ark occupies as much space in Genesis as all the material that went before it, including the days of creation, Adam and Eve, the Garden of Eden, etc. This may be because while the creation of the world and the Garden of Eden were described in a general way, the events of the Flood are described in considerable detail, almost as if someone who had lived at the time of the catastrophe had experienced it as an eyewitness.

It is the first instance in the Bible where exact dimensions, descriptions, and periods of time are given, where geographical points are indicated; the description of how the survival ship was built and even the cargo of the great ship is dealt with. The Ark's exact length, breadth, height, and shape even now are still the guide for modern searchers for the Ark and an opportunity for those who have declared that they have seen it to apply a modern yardstick (in feet) to its ancient measurements (in cubits).

(Although he never visited Ararat, the famous mathematician and scientist Sir Isaac Newton, through a series of calculations determined at the close of the seventeenth century that the Ark was 611.62 feet long, 85.24 feet wide, 51.56 feet in height, between keel and top deck, and weighed, empty, 18231.58 tons.)

With the archaeological knowledge that we now have at our disposal it has become evident that the Judeo-Christian and Moslem accounts of the Deluge can be traced back to prior traditions of earlier races of the Middle East: Sumerians, Babylonians, Assyrians, Egyptians, Hittites, Hurrians, and other ancient peoples who were familiar with the same tradition and who had recorded it at a much earlier period in history. This was not known until the latter part of the nineteenth century, when references to the Flood were found in the ancient cuneiform tablets.

Cuneiform was written by incising letters in the soft clay and then baking it solid, making the tablet virtually timeproof. In fact when some of the ancient cities were conquered and burned the tablets were baked even harder. But this whole record of the Ancient East remained a mystery because the secret of its translation had been lost since the disappearance of the old empires of Babylon, Assyria, and Persia.

The palaces and temples had vanished but the tablets and bricks were still scattered about in great heaps, as well as a few stone monuments. Digging near the mounds unearthed thousands more inscriptions. Quantities of inscribed bricks had been taken from the buried cities by subsequent Arab inhabitants and used for building makeshift houses and compounds. After the disappearances of the old empires the secrets of the meaning of their written language had been lost for thousands of years. Even the names of the cities and their rulers would have been lost had they not been in contact with the Hebrews and mentioned in the Bible. Nobody knew what the strange marks meant. Even European travelers and treasure hunters excavating in the area thought that they were simply an intricate form of decoration.

But in the latter part of the nineteenth century through the efforts principally of British and German archaeologists, aided by the vanity of vanished Persian kings who had had carved self-extolling rock inscriptions in several languages and an Assyrian ruler who had compiled bi- and tri-lingual dictionaries which were found in the ruins of Nineveh, the secrets of the lost languages were revealed and a lost history and literature was brought back to life after 2500 years.

The translations of certain of these tablets have a direct bearing on the story of the Flood and involve a remarkable coincidence. At the time of the great archaeological enthusiasm occasioned by the excavations in the Victorian era of the great buried cities of Mesopotamia, a young English language expert, George Smith, was working on a broken tablet which had been sent back to the British Museum for translation. As he worked he found that the meaning of the text on the tablet seemed to fall into place more easily than usual, almost as if he knew what was coming which, in fact, he did. For he was reading the familiar story of the Great Flood, written in Assyrian. The name of Noah and those of the gods were different but it was obviously the same account. He was unable to finish the translation because the tablet was broken with the rest of it perhaps still in the ruins of Nineveh, covered by the sandy soil of Mesopotamia.

His discovery caused a sensation, as it had been generally assumed that the story of Noah started with the Judeo-Christian version familiar to everyone. Public interest reached such a pitch that the *London Daily Telegraph* organized a field expedition to send George Smith to the ruins of Nineveh where, incredibly, he actually located the missing parts of the tablet to complete the story.

Smith's translation was part of what is now called the Gilgamesh epic, a copy of which had been found in the tablet library of King Ashurbanipal in the ruins of the royal palace in Nineveh. It concerned Gilgamesh, a Sumerian hero figure and demigod common to Sumerian, Babylonian, and Assyrian mythologies, who journies to the Other World in search of the secret of eternal life. There he meets Ut-napishtim, the Sumerian Noah, who tells him the story of the Flood and how he, Ut-napishtim, survived the Deluge by building a great ship in which he saved his family, friends, animals, and plants—"the seed of life" from the flooding waters.

The following extracts from Smith's translation shows how much this account resembles that of Genesis. However, as Egerton Sykes has observed, the fact that the Biblical Flood story resembles that of ancient Babylonia is not due to its having been copied by the Jews but simply that it was a different account of the same happening seen from the viewpoint of another group of survivors.

In the Gilgamesh version, Ut-napishtim is quoted as speaking in the first person to Gilgamesh:

* * *

I caused to embark within the vessel all my family and
    my relations,
The beasts of the field, the cattle of the field, the
    craftsmen, I made them all embark.
I entered the vessel and closed the door . . .
From the foundations of heaven a black cloud
    arose . . .
All that is bright is turned into darkness . . .
The gods feared the flood,
They fled, they climbed into the heaven of Anu,
The gods crouched like a dog on the wall, they lay
    down . . .
For six days and nights
Wind and flood marched on, the hurricane subdued
    the land.
When the seventh day dawned, the hurricane was
    abated, the flood
Which had waged war like an army;
The sea was stilled, the ill wind was calmed, the flood
    ceased.
I beheld the sea, its voice was silent,
And all mankind was turned into mud!
As high as the roofs reached the swamp! . . .
I beheld the world, the horizon of sea;
Twelve measures away an island emerged;
Unto Mount Nisir came the vessel,
Mount Nisir held the vessel and let it not budge . . .
When the seventh day came,
I sent forth a dove, I released it;
It went, the dove, it came back,
As there was no place, it came back.
I sent forth a swallow, it came back,
As there was no place, it came back.
I sent forth a raven, I released it;
It went, the raven, and beheld the subsidence of the
    waters;
It eats, it splashes about, it caws, it comes not back.

Although the dove and the raven are mentioned in the Bible as in the Gilgamesh epic, the Biblical dove, with its olive branch, brings a message of hope while the raven in the Sumerian-Babylonian version stays away from the survival ship since he has found washed up corpses of flood victims to feast upon.

Smith continued his arduous work of translating the Assyrian-Babylonian tablets until he died at the early age of thirty-six, reputedly because he neglected his health and overtaxed his brain. But his success was a reward to him while he lived, especially at the moment of breakthrough when he declared: "I am the first man to read this text after two thousand years of oblivion."

Other tablets (and there are thousands still awaiting translation in the British Museum) revealed, among other matters, more accounts of the Ark. It indicated that the Flood story was well known in the Middle East and was considered a part of history although the main protagonist in each case had a name different from Noah.

The Babylonian historian and priest Berossus wrote that the Flood survivor was Xisuthros (Ziusudra in Babylonian), reputedly the last dynastic king before the Flood. Xisuthros was forewarned by the god Chronos who told him to build a huge ship and to bring into it his family, animals, friends, and supplies. With a commendable historian's regard for archives, Berossus also specifies that Chronos (the Greek name for the god and also the legendary name of the last king of Atlantis), told Xisuthros to collect the records of everything that had been recorded and to bury them at the city of Sippara. (When the Flood was over the royal party went to Sippara and retrieved them.)

Another Assyrio-Babylonian version makes Ubara-tutu or Khasistrata the survivor and attributes to the vessel a length of 600 cubits and a height of 60 and a width also of 60. This enormous size is probably traceable to the Babylonian counting system based on multiples of twelve, still used by the present world for hourly and calendar time and for longitude and latitude and, in the English-speaking world, for linear measurements.

Another version gives the Ark the monstrous dimensions of 5 stadia long and 5 broad—possibly to allow more room for the animals. Occasionally the Mesopotamian version varies the names of Ubaratutu, Khasistrata, Xisuthros, or Baisbarata as the protagonist and some legends specify that the landfall of the Ark was made at Mount Nizir, while another indicates the Gordyene Mountains of Urartu (Armenia). This latter would fit the Ark on Ararat theory, as Mount Ararat was certainly the outstanding and highest mountain of Armenia, which itself was called Urartu in ancient times.

Whether or not the Ark or a great ship did make a landfall on Ararat, the mountain itself by its solitary majesty, its precipitous rise straight up from ground level, its mystery, its air of inaccessibility and danger constitutes a convincing indication to anyone looking at it of its peculiar place in the history of humanity.

For the townspeople and herdsmen living near Mount Ararat, place names and natural features provide a vivid memory of the Great Flood. Nakhichevan, now in Soviet Armenia, means "the landing place" and Echmiadzin, where reputed pieces of the Ark are kept in the monastery, means "the descent" or "those who descended." Arghuri (Ahora) signifies "the planting of the vine" referring to the grapevine planted by Noah after leaving the Ark. On the Iranian side of the frontier a town called Temanin means "the eight," a supposed reference to the number of persons, Noah and his family, who survived the Flood. A village about eighteen miles from Mount Ararat, in the vicinity of the buried Ark is called Mahşer, meaning "doomsday," a pointed reminder of the catastrophic punishment of the world. And researcher David Fasold, while sketching a facsimile of the buried Ark, found that a place name near the Ark formation was called Kargakonmaz meaning "the raven won't land"—a recognizable reference to the raven returning to the Ark after searching unsuccessfully for land.

A well on the northeastern side of the mountain commemorates St. Jacob's laborious attempts to climb the mountain in search of the Ark. The water in "Jacob's Well" is supposed to have come from a spring which miraculously appeared where St. Jacob had rested his head. The spot where the animals were loaded on the Ark is still pointed out as the place where they were freed by Noah.

The fact that the legend of the Ark appears in a recognizable form in various pre-Biblical Mesopotamian written accounts makes it considerably older than previously supposed. It is older than the recorded history to which archaeology has been able to assign a date. Since the translation of the cuneiform tablets more than a hundred years ago we know that various races of the ancient Middle East shared versions of the same legend. The memory of the world before the Flood was part of their ancient history. King Ashurbanipal of Assyria, whose library provided the basis for the translation of the Flood legend, is reported to have once said to his courtiers in a discussion about ancient legends and the world before the Flood:

* * *

There—in the desert long ago—there were
mighty cities whose very walls have disappeared,
but we still have records of their languages on our
tablets. . . .

Was the Biblical Flood account itself an adaptation
of legends already thousands of years old? Perhaps
Abraham had heard of it when he was in Ur, or Hebrew
scholars had become familiar with it and later adapted it
during the Babylonian captivity, or Moses, the presumed writer of the Torah and therefore of Genesis,
had heard of the great world flood when he lived in
Egypt. Mohammed, when writing in the Koran the vivid
description of the flooding waters, perhaps had learned
about the Flood from a selection of sources including
the pre-Islamic civilizations along the coast of Arabia.
But there is ample evidence that there was a common
memory of a phenomenon that affected all areas of the
planet and was therefore remembered by tribes and nations that did not know of each others' existence and
reported their own experiences in local context. In the
Greco-Roman legend the survivors were Deucalion and
his wife Pyhrra, who were saved with their children and
a collection of wild and domestic animals in a vessel built
like a great box. After the vessel ran aground on Mount
Parnassus they repopulated the world on the advice of
the gods by throwing stones behind them as they walked
down the mountain, the stones becoming men or
women according to the sex of the thrower.

According to the prehistoric records of India, the
Puranas and the *Mahabharata*, Manu and seven companions were the survivors (as in Noah, the number eight!)
and an avatar of the god Vishnu, in the form of a great
fish, pulled Manu's ship (the fish had a convenient horn

on the end of its head for towing) to Mount Himavet in the northern mountains of India.

There were two traditions of a Great Flood in Egypt (as opposed to the annual floodings of the Nile), one mythological and one in the careful recording style of the scribes. In the mythological version the cat goddesses Bast and Sekmet had been sent by the gods to destroy humanity and by a series of catastrophes and bloodshed were well on the way to doing so—until the gods realized that without humanity they would have no worshipers. The gods then sent a flood of beer into the waters and after they had lapped up enough to make them fall asleep, caused the cat goddesses to forget about their mission.

In a somewhat more logical version, as reported by the Coptic historian Masudi, Surid, one of the Egyptian pre-dynastic kings who lived before the Flood, dreamed that a great flood and fire would come from and during the apogee of the constellation Leo. King Surid then ordered that the two greatest pyramids, Khufu (*Cheops* in Greek) and Khafra, be built "recording on their walls all the secret sciences together with the star positions and also all that was known of arithmetic and geometry . . . so that they would be as a witness for the benefit of those who would eventually understand them."

It is known from Greek and Roman times that the outer casings of the two pyramids were covered with inscriptions. The casings were removed in the Middle Ages and used for the construction of buildings in Cairo, including specifically the mosque of Ibu Tulum, which may therefore contain unusual archaeological, but still hidden, information. It is interesting to note, in regard to the possibility of its having been built before the Flood,

*that within the larger of the two pyramids, that of
Khufu, there is an inexplicable high-water mark in the
Queen's Chamber.*

In old Persian traditions the Flood hero was called
Yima and, more convivially than the other Noahs, he
invited one thousand couples to share his refuge. His
Ark was not a ship but a subterranean "bunker" called a
vara, made of clay, three stories deep with wide central
avenues "a horse-run long." His companions were judi-
ciously screened for evil customs, leprosy, and even un-
even teeth. Yima and his healthy companions remained
underground while fires, floods, and earthquakes shook
the world and when the catastrophe was over they ascended again to the surface of the earth.

The tribes of pre-Christian Europe had memories
of a Great Flood which happened long before Christianity and before the legend of Noah was introduced
by missionaries from the Greco-Roman world. Some of
these legends deal, as did the Persian version, with a
combination of flood and fire and sometimes not with
flooding from rain but with a spontaneous rising of the
ocean and the permanent sinking undersea of coastal
lands along the Atlantic littoral.

In pre-Christian Ireland, a sudden oceanic rise
caused Queen Ceseair and her court to take ship and
sail through the flood for seven and a half years. They
never did get back to Ireland because it was so washed
by the sea that no one settled there for 200 years after
the Flood. The Great Flood is remembered in the Welsh
annals *The Third Catastrophe of Britain* and the survivors
were Dwyfan and Dwyfach.

The Norsemen and Germanic peoples of the
north, in remembering the shakings of the earth and

the retreat of the sea and its return in tidal waves, express the occurrence in terms of a trial of strength between the boastful god Thor and the King of the Frost Giants. When Thor was in the house of the Frost Giant the king asked Thor if he could drink to the bottom of a large flagon of beer, a test that Thor accepted with pleasure. But after a godlike effort he had been able to lower the level only a little. The Frost Giant then asked Thor if he were strong enough to lift a nearby cat and Thor, however mightily he tried, succeeded only in budging it a little. As Thor left, somewhat shaken by his lack of capacity for beer and diminishing lifting strength, he was told that the drinking horn was attached to the sea itself (which had fallen away from the northern coast) and that the cat's tail was connected with the Midguard serpent whose tail encircles and sustains the earth which, at the same time that Thor was trying to lift the cat, had been shaken by such enormous earthquakes that even the gods became afraid.

A more vivid Scandinavian description of an ancient catastrophe is recalled in the Icelandic saga, the *Edda:*

> Mountains dash together . . .
> And heaven is split in two,
> The sun grows dead—
> The earth sinks into the sea,
> The bright stars vanish
> Fires rage and raise their flames
> As high as heaven.

Other pre-Christian cultures on the western coasts of Europe still retain the memory of cities suddenly flooded and permanently covered by the sea and Atlantic islands sinking with their entire populations, except for a few survivors, under great tidal waves. While these legends of pagan times do not specify any particular survivors, the ancient Gauls claimed to the Roman conquerors that their ancestors were survivors of a former island in the Atlantic Ocean.

Even today, in a Breton folk memory of the sudden rising of the ocean, there persists the legend on the north Atlantic coast of France that on certain days the bells of sunken cathedrals can be heard echoing up from the sea bottom where the submerged cities of Lyonesse and Ys still testify to the flooding of the ocean that covered them and never did subside.

The Flood legends of the New World constitute something of a mystery, commented upon by the first Spanish military explorers, who were puzzled as to how the American Indian tribes and nations possessed essentially the same Flood legends, paralleling so closely that of the Bible. The immediate reaction of the Spanish priests was that all resemblances to Christianity and the Bible among the Indians, including baptism, the symbol of the Cross, etc., were a tactic of the Devil to spread confusion. Moreover, since there is no apparent reference in the Bible or Church commentaries to the Indian tribes, the Spanish missionaries deduced that they might be the ten lost tribes of Israel. Other commentators suspected that the Flood legend had been imported through prior contact between the Old World and the New—although these terms are something of a misnomer since the New World as we now know is fully as old as the so-called Old World, certainly in terms of animals and, perhaps, of man.

From Mexico to the far north and again south through mountains, jungles, and deserts to the southern tip of South America, Amerindians all remembered a catastrophe; usually an encompassing flood although often augmented by earthquakes, eruptions of volcanoes and rising and falling of mountains. There are even more independent legends of the Flood in the Americas than in Europe and the Middle East. The Noah figure of the Amerindians has a variety of different names or, when a specific name is not mentioned, then the name of the whole tribe is used. A frequent means of escape consisted of typically Indian artifacts such as large covered canoes, rafts, hollowed tree trunks and, in the case of Eskimos, many kayaks lashed together. The Tlingit legend from Alaska tells of bears and wolves trying to get aboard the escaping canoes as the waters rose, and being beaten back by the paddles of the rowers. Some legends, such as that of the Toltecs of Central America, specify a great boxlike chest, similar to the one described in the ancient Greek version.

A Huron legend deals with the Great Father of the Indian tribes surviving with his family and selected animals on a large covered raft. During their stay on the Ark the animals (who then had the power of speech) complained so constantly that after landing the power of speech was taken from them. In Inca legend the Flood was predicted by a talking llama that led his owner to a high mountain in the Andes where other people and animals, already warned, waited out the Flood. The high mountain of refuge for the Navajos was said to be the San Francisco Peak near Flagstaff, Arizona. The Navajo survivors had no boats, but simply fled up the peak, taking their sheep with them. When the Flood drained away into the Grand Canyon, they returned to their land.

Flood accounts of the Aztecs and other Central

American peoples give several names for the main survivor, such as Coxcox, Tezpi, and Teocipactli, and mention that the vessel, a large raft, was made of cypress root, a wood that has been suggested as what was meant by the gopherwood of the Bible. The birds that were sent out but did not return were vultures that stayed to eat the drowned people and animals that had washed up together with wreckage, while the bird that came back to the Ark with a leaf was the small hummingbird, enabling Coxcox (or Tezpi or Teocipactli) to make landfall on the crooked mountain of Colhuacan. When the flood receded a great pyramid was built at Cholula to provide a refuge from future floods. The pyramid is still there, and the next and final world catastrophe, as predicted by the Aztecs, the end of the world by fire, will fall due in our own system of counting time, around the end of this present century.

Like the old Persian legend, some survivors escaped the Flood without the aid of a boat. According to the Chibcha records of Colombia the hero, Bochica, and his wife escaped up a high mountain by ascending on camels (once extant in South America, but not for the last few thousand years).

A number of Indian traditions contain references to catastrophes of earthquakes and fire from the sky in addition to floods. The Maya written records such as the *Popul Vuh* and the *Book of Chilam Balaam* tell of survivors who hid in deep caves until the floods, fire, and earthquakes ceased. Huge underground caves are plentiful in Yucatán and some of these contain enormous carved stone statues of animals, some with human heads, dissimilar to any known Mayan artifacts. There are visible indications that some of these caves have been underwater long enough to leave vestiges of mollusks and other sea fauna on the carved figures.

A voyaging white man is mentioned in the Mandan tribal legend as having come from the east in a large covered canoe in which he had escaped from the Flood and had found new land uncovered by waters in the west. When he landed he was joined by survivors who had waited out the Flood in tunnels and had ascertained that the waters had receded by sending out a mouse which, by not returning to the tunnel, indicated that the waters had subsided.

The Hopi tribe of the western United States has kept more detailed records of the past than other tribal groups. There is a reference in their legends to a flood without rain caused by waves higher than mountains coming from the sea and rolling over the land: ". . . The continents broke apart and sank under the waves." The Hopis survived on the highest mountain while ". . . all the proud cities were covered by the sea."

The lack of any mention of rain as the immediate cause of a sudden Great Flood exists in a number of legends of ancient America. The tradition of tremendous waves *from the ocean* enveloping the land, coupled with seismic disturbances, may be a racial memory of a world catastrophe of which the Flood was not the cause but rather the effect.

Flood accounts of Babylon and Assyria describe waterspouts and tidal waves along with the rain as if the bottom of the ocean were itself disturbed. Accounts from the Greco-Roman world mention shakings of the earth that precipitated cities into the sea as well as the one in their own prehistory that separated Sicily from the Italian mainland.

The Bible, in describing the Flood (Genesis 7:11) suggests that water was rising from turbulence within the depths of the ocean as well as coming from the rain: ". . . on the same day were all the fountains of the great deep broken up, and the windows of heaven were opened. . . ." The Koran is even more evocative of earth changes as in Sura VII: ". . . the earth's surface seethed . . . the Ark moved . . . amid waves like mountains."

In Chinese legends there are two Flood accounts, one coming across Asia from the west, brought by the Turkic peoples of Central Asia, and therefore following the Koranic references to the Flood of Nūh, or Nu-Hwa, as it has been adapted into Chinese. When the Christian missionaries brought the Bible into China and found that the Middle Eastern version of the story of the Flood was already known, they understandably interpreted this as an additional proof of the Flood story, even to the name of Noah.

But there is a completely different version of a flood and catastrophe that comes from the ancient Chinese Encyclopedia. Here Noah is named Fo-Hsi, and the circumstances are considerably different and of cosmic scope.

The early Jesuit missionaries to China were referred by Chinese scholars to the 4320 *volume* work, compiled by Imperial Edict, called the *Ch'in-ting-ku-chin-t'su-shu-shi-ch'eng* and designed to contain "all knowledge." The reference to a catastrophe and flood is impressive:

> . . . The Earth was shaken to its foundations. The sky sank lower toward the north. The sun, moon, and stars changed their motions. The Earth fell to pieces and the waters in its bosom rushed upward with violence and overflowed the Earth. Man had rebelled against the high gods and the system of the Universe was in disorder. The planets altered their courses and the grand harmony of the Universe and nature was disturbed. . . .

*   *   *

While some legends state that the whole earth was covered by water which fell from the heavens, others
specify that waves covered the land or that the land
sank. If the catastrophe remembered by all peoples was
caused, as some scientific commentators on pre-history
have suggested, by a collision between the earth and a
giant meteorite or any other event capable of shaking
the earth on its axis or even of permanently modifying
the rotation of the earth, the oceans would have risen in
great tidal waves and temporarily covered most of the
land areas. Thus parts of the coastline and the oceanic
islands would have sunk or risen, depending on the
action of volcanic faults, and new mountain ranges
would have been forced up. The civilization that man
had developed before the Flood would have vanished,
swept away, buried under the enfolding earth, or sunk
beneath the sea, leaving only certain ruins made of giant
stones unidentifiable in recorded history. Certain ships
might have survived and, caught in the waves of the
Flood, been washed up into the crevasses of the mountains and high plateaus, borne by the giant tsunamis
that swept the world. The Ark of Noah may be one of
these.

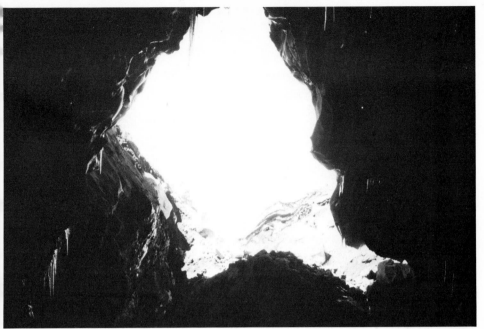

Photograph taken pointing upward toward the sky from the inside of a cave whose entrance is shown on Mıh Tepe Glacier. Caves on the higher slopes are seasonally covered with thick ice from the glaciers. The caves on the lower slopes often contain bears, wolves, wild dogs, and poisonous snakes. *Ahmet Ali Arslan*

Devil's Rock seen from east to west. This is one of the several formations mistaken for the Ark by ancient and modern travelers. Küp Lake and the Parrot Glacier are on the other side of this rock formation. *Ahmet Ali Arslan*

Climbers on Mount Ararat have noted that it is possible to hear rushing waters flowing under the glaciers while camping on the mountain and trying to sleep. These waters melting under the glaciers disappear and apparently go underground at a lower point before reappearing on the Ararat Plain in streams or lakes. They are the source of Kara Su (Black Water) and the Süreyya Çesmesi (the Fountains of Soraya), a graceful tribute to the former queen of Iran. © *Jay Bitzer*

Dust-covered Black Glacier over Ahora. The smaller summit can be seen in the background. *Ahmet Ali Arslan*

The white puff of smoke shown here at 9 A.M. is the beginning of a fog which will soon encompass the entire upper part of Mount Ararat. *Ahmet Ali Arslan*

Parrot Glacier from the west, with advancing clouds about to cover it. Mountain climbers have frequently been lost because of these sudden fogs and others have been killed by breaking through thin ice into crevasses because they could not see where they were going. *Ahmet Ali Arslan*

Ark shape at Mahşer with lines based on the use of subsurface radar purportedly showing position of sections, living quarters, or enclosures for animals on the Ark. Tapes run east to west and north to south. *Ahmet Ali Arslan*

The buried Ark with metal-detector equipment in place. The break in the presumed port side of the ship formation can be seen in the center bulwark shown in the picture. *Ahmet Ali Arslan*

Unusual stone formation which may be a part of the buried Ark and which may have separated from it during its slide from a higher level to its present location. The stratified lines on the object indicate, according to Fasold's theory, that the Ark was an enormous reed structure over which a form of cement was poured to construct and waterproof the great vessel. It is further theorized that this cement is a mistranslation of the gopherwood mentioned in the Bible and should be the bituminous cement mix expressed in the ancient Akkadian language by the consonants K-F-R. *David Fasold*

The man in the picture is seated on a stone anchor, one of several found near Mount Ararat. Two of these have been found north of Koran and two more are kept in the village. These large stone anchors were used on ancient ships, and their presence on dry land far from the sea is a further indication that the plain on which these anchors lie was once the bottom of the sea. *David Fasold*

Side view of buried Ark showing abrupt rising of formation from ground, a rise which may have increased (or the ground has perhaps sunk) since the object was first discovered. *Ahmet Ali Arslan*

Close-up view of one of the discovered sea anchors showing the broken hole through which a cable was passed to secure the dragging anchor. Other similar anchors have been found underwater or on the beaches of the Mediterranean, on the Atlantic coasts of Spain, France, and Ireland, and off the coast of California. *David Fasold*

Investigation of area alleged to be the inside remains of the starboard bow of the buried Ark. The raised center formation corresponds to the second bulkhead back from the bow, serving as an upper-deck support beam in line with the port side. The opening to the left may indicate where a support column has fallen out. The left line held by the expedition member is a measuring tape, while the second tape is a survey ribbon showing a line of buried metal readings, presumably spikes or long nails 12 or 15 inches apart. *David Fasold*

8

Dry Seabeds and Sunken Lands

Ever since 2500 years ago when the Greek historian Herodotus noted the presence of seashells in the desert near the pyramids, other observers have made a number of references to the invasion of the sea over the lands of the Middle East. In ancient and medieval times this was generally attributed to the Great Flood although, in fairly modern times starting with the twentieth century, there has been considerable scientific skepticism directed against Biblical material as a valid historical reference.

But even in modern times vestiges of prolonged flooding are still noticeable in the Middle East, especially in the Ararat area. Seashells have been found on Mount Ararat at 10,000-feet elevations. Salt clusters at 7000-feet elevation indicate a gradual drying up of seawater which was once present there. Pillow lava is found on Mount Ararat as well as on the bottom of the Atlantic Ocean and the presence of pillow lava indicates that lava extruded above sea level has been submerged underwater for a certain period of time. There are saltwater herring, apparently cut off from their home in the ocean, still living in Lake Urmia in Eastern Turkey far from the sea. The geologist Dr. Evan Hansen has called attention to the strange rock formations in Eastern Turkey which show traces of the "braided flow of water" where former high ground was washed away leaving narrow pinnacles remaining as sharp islands showing where the former ground level existed, a phenomenon also familiar in the southwestern United States.

A striking discovery involving proof of a prolonged flood that had occurred in Mesopotamia thousands of years ago was produced during an archaeological excavation in Ur, one of the world's oldest cities, carried out by archaeologist Leonard Woolley in the late 1920s.

Woolley, who had made a series of unusual finds demonstrating the high level attained by the early civilization of Sumeria at extremely ancient epochs, had the original idea of digging a shaft straight down through the ruins of Ur. He wished to establish, by digging through successive layers of cultures, the first stratum or starting point of Sumerian civilization.

As the excavation down the narrow shaft proceeded (ignoring lateral shards on either side) all sorts of artifacts were unearthed from stages of culture going back to a period thousands of years B.C. Then the finds stopped and subsequent diggings revealed nothing but mud. Nevertheless Woolley ordered the digging through the mud to continue and after ten feet another layer of artifacts appeared denoting another type of civilization or civilizations that had flourished before the influx of mud.

As reported by William E. Shirer (*Twentieth Century Journey*), who interviewed Woolley on the site, Woolley was discussing the strange discovery with his staff when his wife, Katherine, also a dedicated archaeologist, joined the group. When Woolley asked her if she had any opinion of what the mud interval could be she immediately replied, "Well, of course. It's the Flood!"

Following excavations showed the mud stratum to be even more pronounced—twelve feet thick—indicating that it was not a seasonal flood but a prolonged inundation before the waters drained away. Woolley concluded that the floodwaters were originally twenty-five feet deep—almost exactly the information, translated from cubits, contained in Genesis: ". . . Fifteen cubits upward did the waters prevail. . . ."

Great and prolonged floods were not limited to the Middle East. Skeletons of whales have been found in the Himalayas, the world's highest range, and fish bones and clamshells have been found on Mount Ararat.

Near the mysterious ruins of Tiahuanaco, Bolivia, more than two miles high in the Andes Range, there is a salt line traceable on the surrounding mountains. There are indications that the city in the mountains was once a large port at sea level and that Lake Titicaca may represent a former link with the ocean. A. Posnanski, an Austrian archaeologist who became director of the National Museum of Bolivia and the Ica Institute of Anthropology, has estimated Tiahuanaco's age at 15,000 years before present. Possibly constructed before a worldwide catastrophe that may have thrust up the geologically recent Andes to their present height while sinking, through the process known as isostasis, other parts of the earth beneath the sea temporarily or permanently. As for the age of Tiahuanaco, it is perhaps pertinent to recall that there is depicted on pottery recovered there representations of vanished species including the toxodon, a prehistoric animal that once lived in South America and which was apparently still extant when Tiahuanaco was built.

An unusual racial memory of an encompassing flood which covered a great land mass and from which a handful of survivors climbed to the highest peaks, which then became islands in the ocean, was told to early French and Spanish navigators exploring west into the Atlantic almost a hundred years before Columbus' first voyage. The Canary Islands were the first Central Atlantic islands to be discovered and the indigenous inhabitants believed that they were the sole survivors on earth from a flood that had happened thousands of years before.

The inhabitants of the Canary Islands were white skinned, of tall and muscular stature, and many were blond-haired and blue-eyed. They were officially discovered in 1395 by Jean de Béthencourt, a French nobleman in the service of Spain. When the Spanish landed they could not communicate with the natives, who spoke no language known to the Spaniards. When the islanders had learned enough Spanish to communicate they told the surprised Spanish visitors that they could not understand where the men and ships had come from as they believed that the Great Flood had drowned everyone in the world except themselves. Once, they said, their ancestors had lived in a large land with great cities, fertile plains, and rivers, but a flood had covered it, and only a few people who had been able to flee to the high mountains had survived. The islands where they now were living once were the mountaintops of their vanished homeland. The waters of the flood (unlike those of the Biblical Flood) never receded but (and they pointed to the surrounding Atlantic Ocean) were still there.

This curious tradition with its suggestion of Atlantis, the Flood, a civilization destroyed by the waters, and survivors who fled to the mountains, was never sufficiently researched by the Spanish conquerors who, within a short time, annihilated the native population in a series of wars. Their language too was lost although some of the Spaniards remembered that a few words resembled the names of the ancient Greek gods, including Chronos, a traditional name for one of the kings of Atlantis.

The Sahara, once a tree-covered and well-watered area, has dried up within the last 10,000 to 20,000 years although underground rivers still flow beneath it. Ancient "pre-desert" rock paintings found on cliffs and in caves of the Tassili Mountains depict the life of a vanished people who lived there before the waters rolled in and flooded the land and then evaporated and left it a desert. It is possible that the same flood broke down the barrier between Europe and Africa at Gibraltar, letting in the ocean waters which transformed a series of lakes and valleys into the Mediterranean Sea. Biblical references to certain great rivers not presently identified (Genesis 2) may refer to rivers now covered by the Mediterranean or the Black Sea.

Egerton Sykes had suggested that the Black Sea, the Caspian Sea, and Lake Aral were once connected with a great sea of which the eastern shore was the Western Gobi and that the hypothetical Ark did not sail from the south (as suggested in Babylonian tradition, which tells of the Ark's construction in Maala, near Aden, Southern Arabia), but from this great sea to the northeast of which the former sea bottom is now largely desert.

It is possible to establish the variation in the rising and falling of the earth's surface by the unusual location of sandy or pebble beaches, which normally follow the coastlines of islands and continents. Beaches and remains of sea life high over sea level or sandy beaches deep under the ocean are clear indications that the sea level has changed, since beaches are formed by waves breaking on the shore. We find beach sand in deserts throughout the world and raised beaches, hundreds of feet high, in Alaska, California, Newfoundland, Norway, and other places in the northern part of the northern hemisphere.

Large parts of the earth's surface have been covered by the Flood and not yet relinquished by the waters. Mammoth, mastodon, and human bones and tools of prehistoric man have been brought up from the sea floor of the Dogger Bank in the North Sea and beaches have been found at the bottom of the Atlantic Ocean near the Azores.

These beaches, once the shorelines of now submerged islands and land masses, appear to have been precipitated to the bottom of the ocean by sudden volcanic action. The late oceanographer Dr. M. Ewing, heading a dredging expedition, found beach sand at a depth of three and a half miles as well as granite rocks marked by previous glacial striations. What appear to be stone ruins of sunken cities still lie on the floor of the Mediterranean, off the African coast, near the Azores and Madeira islands, and on the continental shelves near Cuba and the Bahamas. A massive and apparently man-made wall off the coast of Peru has sunk to a depth of a mile and a half into the Nazca Deep.

A number of theorists believe that what happened to the earth at the time of catastrophe was violent enough to change the tilt of the earth upon its axis, thereby unleashing the oceans over the land, dislodging and melting the ice from the north, and causing seismic, through seismic upheaval, land areas to rise and sink in many parts of the earth. But the climatic change, however, that occurred at the sudden end of the last glaciation is not a theory but an obvious reality and as such accepted by science.

Much of the glacial ice pack that formerly covered the northern regions of the earth is now found in Antarctica, covering the Antarctic continent to a depth of up to two miles and still increasing. If this ice pack should melt at some future time humanity would experience another disastrous flood, considering that 80 percent of the world's peoples live in areas no higher than 100 feet above sea level.

Antarctica's topography furnishes us with unique proof of the catastrophic changes which occurred at the time of the Deluge, as well as the suggestion of man's progress in civilization before the Flood. Antarctica itself was not discovered by modern man until the 1820s, some years after Captain Cook had failed to find it and deduced that it did not exist. Previously it had been thought that extensive land must exist at the South Pole to balance the continents, but sailing in uncharted seas was difficult because lines of longitude had not been determined and were not determined until late in the reign of George III, at the beginning of the nineteenth century.

However, certain ancient Greek or Phoenician maps, probably rescued from the library of Alexandria and other libraries of antiquity since destroyed, showed a continent and details of land areas at the southern edge of the world. Therefore, for lack of anything better to show on world maps, these ancient concepts were copied and printed before there was any proof that Antarctica existed. This was done on the Buache map (1737), the Finaeus map (1532), and others. And a surviving sixth part of a world map, the Piri Re'is map (1513), also copied from ancient Greek and Phoenician maps, indicated a connection between Argentina and an Antarctic land area which *would be* exact if a map had been drawn before the ocean increased in depth, filled with water left by the Deluge.

The late Charles Hapgood *(Maps of the Ancient Sea Kings; The Path of the Pole)*, a professor at Keene State College, New Hampshire, made the discovery that the Piri Re'is map demonstrated the use of spherical geometry and the use of longitude. For years he studied this and other ancient maps filed away in the Library of Congress and became convinced that ancient mariners visited and explored Antarctica before the last great climatic change that determined the climate zones of the post-Flood world.

Hapgood was fortified in his theories by a series of geographical discoveries which corroborated the "fanciful" concepts of the ancient maps. The shorelines of Antarctica which the maps showed were not those of the present maritime maps. However, they were true shorelines nevertheless as they showed Antarctica as it would be without the ice. The rivers indicated on the ancient maps are now covered with glaciers, still following the course of the prehistoric rivers and, most surprising of all, Antarctica was shown on the ancient maps to be composed of two islands—not one land mass as previously supposed. This information, found to be exact by an international expedition in 1968, was evidently known to explorers at a time now estimated as 8000–10,000 B.C.

The seafarers who visited Antarctica were from the world before the Flood. Under the deep glacial ice there may yet exist great ships contemporary with or even previous to Noah's Ark.

9

Animal Species That Disappeared With the Flood

The gathering, loading onto the Ark, and feeding of male and female examples of all living things (except fishes?) by Noah and his family for a period of more than half a year has long been a favorite subject for ancient and modern painters and illustrators. It has also furnished a source of derision for those who actively oppose belief in the Flood and the Ark.

Nonbelievers in this ancient legend frequently point out a number of inconsistencies, any one of which is significant, in their opinion, to discredit the survival voyage of the animals on the Ark.

As some of these questions are difficult to answer in terms of known experience, the answers following each rhetorical question are compiled from opinions based on faith in the letter of the Bible and in miracles that are contrary to scientific logic that nevertheless become logical when accompanied by faith.

*   *   *

137

How were the animals gathered? How was it possible for animals living in far parts of the earth, like the kangaroo, to get to the Ark?

Each pair of animals, male and female, was guided there by the Spirit of God.

Even if the Ark were as large as described in Genesis (6:15), how could the small crew composed of Noah's family possibly feed them? And why did not the carnivorous animals eat the smaller ones?

Once the animals were on the Ark they went into a state of hibernation and did not need food.

In Genesis (7) it mentions that "every clean beast" and "the fowls also of the air" were taken aboard in groups of seven while the "beasts that are not clean" were restricted to one pair of each kind. Why this distinction?

God wished to help Noah and his family after landing by providing them with extra domestic animals.

If the serpent had been cursed by God, why was it allowed on the Ark?

The snake and his descendants already had been punished (Genesis 3:14).

We know the dimensions of the Ark as given in the Bible. How would it be possible to fit within the comparatively small space the many thousands of kinds of animals and birds that exist?

The Bible does not necessarily mean every kind of animal and bird, but only the genus. Many of the species and subspecies have developed since the Flood. Two horses, for example, were enough to ensure the different species of horses, two deer for the many species of deer, two lions or tigers for the many types of felines, two dogs for the numerous examples of canine variation.

While life on board the Ark during the Flood is treated but briefly in Genesis, a series of minor traditions has been handed down over thousands of years. One such version tells of an increase in mice and rats among the grain stores. God therefore caused the lion to sneeze and the lion sneezed a cat, which immediately set off after the rodents. (As the cat is never mentioned in the Bible, this particular legend may be an attempt to justify his existence.)

Pictorial representations of the Ark continue to be popular in the modern world, not only in children's books but for use in jocular captions in popular humor magazines. The Ark is always shown with long-necked giraffes, huge elephants, and other large animals difficult to fit in an Ark, crowding the gunwales as the ship sails over an endless sea or is stuck on a mountaintop.

To doubt any part of the Ark legend is not to doubt the Flood or the survival of individuals who, living through the catastrophe, felt that they had been chosen to survive—and perhaps they had. It is also logical to presume that a figurative Noah would wish to save as many of his family and livestock and as much of his food and seed supply as possible to start a new life after the Flood.

And other Noahs, differing in name, place, and individual experience, must have survived in ships or refuges in high places in other parts of the world. Varying legends about these other Noahs have been kept alive by their descendants for a hundred centuries.

Our own legend of Noah and the Flood, starting in the Middle East, was eventually carried, through Christianity, to all parts of the world. As the Noah legend spread it encountered memories of a catastrophic Flood already held by peoples in ancient Europe, Asia, Africa, the Americas, and the islands of the Pacific. All of these legends coincided with the Biblical record in principle although not in local detail. Other Flood stories mention a variety of animals—the llamas and other animals that followed the South American Indians up the high Andes, other animals that were transported to safety in huge rafts or taken into high caves in the mountains.

Other Flood legends mention a variety of animals: bears, wolves, llamas, camels, horses, and mice. Genesis, with the exception of the differentiation between "every clean beast" and "beasts that are not clean" and the dove and the raven, does not mention any individual animal, nor any kind of animal in existence *before* the Flood whose species did not survive.

The point has been raised as to why there is no mention in the Bible of the lumbering monsters of prehistoric eras, whose dimensions we now know and whose general features we can reconstruct. When great bones of prehistoric animals were first found by chance in deep pits being excavated in Europe some churchmen held that the strange bones had been created along with the rocks and stones underground in the earth. Others, more logically, assumed that these were the remains of unidentified animals that had disappeared during or before the Flood. We now know through calculations of the earth's strata where the bones are found that the great dinosaurs vanished 55,000,000 to 60,000,000 years before man appeared—probably as a result of the planets passing through a cosmic cloud that altered the climate of the earth.

But it is the Bible itself, in dealing with the geologically recent Deluge of Noah and the drowning of the animals at the time of the Flood, that gives us the most striking proof of a worldwide catastrophic event of which the Flood was a part, another indication of the unexpected concordance of the Biblical text with recent zoological information. For while Biblical tradition does not specify a date for the Flood, apart from references to life-spans of the patriarchs, it clearly indicates that man had already existed long enough to develop a way of life or civilization whose customs were displeasing to the Deity (Genesis 6:17).

Many types of animal life, species and genera, did effectively disappear at the time that something caused the glaciers to melt and the oceans to overflow, earthquakes, and the rapid, almost instantaneous change of climate. These were the animal species which, speaking figuratively, were not successful in sending representative couples to the Ark and which disappeared from biological history 11,000 to 12,000 years ago. Something very deadly modified all forms of animal life at this time, causing whole species to vanish in gigantic hecatombs and the species that survived to undergo a sort of instant evolution.

These drowned animals have been found in vast numbers in high mountain caves and crevasses and in great boneyards in various parts of the world in places where they had congregated in a vain attempt to escape the Flood. Dr. J. Manson Valentine, paleontologist and zoologist who has visited a number of these deposits, points out the wide scope of the animal death traps of 11,000 years ago:

*   *   *

In Wales, Devonshire and various places in Southern England we find, filling crevasses in the hills, massive deposits of splintered bones of hyenas, hippopotami, elephants, Arctic bears and a host of more familiar animals, a phenomenon repeated in a number of sites in Western Europe. In rock crevasses on Mount Genay in France were wedged the bones of rhinoceros, elephants, lions and wild oxen; in the Swiss Alps, crocodiles, giant ostriches and polar bears.

In the Dakota boneyards the pushed-together bones of camels and horses along with other animals difficult to identify have consolidated through pressure into huge bone blocks. In Nebraska the boneyards include rhinoceros and giant pigs. In the La Brea pits of California there are giant sloths, camels, lions, horses, peacocks and prehistoric buffaloes.

In a sinkhole in the Florida Everglades a huge curved tusk protruding out of the mud was found to be connected to a skeleton of a giant mastodon dead at least eleven thousand years. Around it were crowded camels, horses, tigers and sloths with an incalculable number of other species under the muck. . . .

In Northern Siberia the Lyakoff Islands are strewn so thickly with mammoth bones that they were first called the Bone Islands. The bones not only cover the islands but, as if the mammoths were crowding on them in an attempt to escape the Flood, the massed bones of drowned animals form underwater banks around the islands.

Dr. Immanuel Velikovsky, in commenting on the world catastrophe that caused the doom of so many animals, noticed the suddenness of their deaths and the mixture of species in his book *Earth in Upheaval.*

> . . . in the hills of Montreal and New Hampshire and in Michigan, five and six hundred feet above sea level, bones of whales have been found. In many places on earth—on all continents—bones of sea animals and polar land animals and tropical animals have been found in great melées; so also in the Cumberland Cave in Maryland, in the Chou Kou Tien fissure in China, and also in Germany and Denmark. Hippopotami and ostriches were found together with seals and reindeer . . . from the Arctic to the Antarctic . . . in the high mountains and in the deep seas—we find innumerable signs of great upheavals. . . .

The mammoths of Siberia had been kept in deep freeze ever since the sudden flood buried them under a sea of mud which later froze and preserved them. For thousands of years ivory has been gathered from this great graveyard of the mammoths—ivory which would not have been usable or salable if it were dry or cracked and not perfectly preserved. The preservation of the bodies of many of these mammoths, complete with hair, tusks, flesh, organs, and sometimes even eyeballs, led the native Siberian tribesmen to believe that the great beasts were still alive, burrowing under the snow. The Tungus word *mamut* from which we get "mammoth" means "a burrower." Professor Charles Hapgood in his book *The Path of the Pole* has pointed out that the contents of the stomach of one quick-frozen Siberian mammoth showed that the animal had been eating buttercups when the water and mud tidal wave engulfed it—certainly an incongruous food supply for what we now know of the climate of Northern Siberia. The speed of the "quick-freeze" that overcame some of these mammoths is indicated by the ice crystals found *inside* their lungs.

All these animal species that seem anachronistic to the environments where they were found died in the Flood or in the accompanying climate change. With the end of the Third Glaciation the great Irish elk, the cave bear, the giant auroch, and the dire wolf disappeared in Europe. At the same time, in South America, horses, elephants, lions, giant sloths, toxodons (a hippopotamus type of animal), and glyptodons (an enormous armadillo) became extinct. In Southeastern Asia thirty species of elephants disappeared and all but two species of rhinoceros.

A pertinent comment regarding the extinction of so many species was made by Charles Darwin during his investigations in South America when he observed that most of the extinct South American animals were contemporaneous with the seashells found on land.

The possibility that man existed in South America at the time of the extinction of many animal species through a flood is made evident by the carvings of lions, rhinoceros, and camels on rocks in the high plateaus of the Andes and jungles of South America, made thousands of years before the first Amerindian civilization of which we have record.

The Great Flood has been described in the oldest chronicles of ancient cultures. It has left watermarks over the surface of the world. The floodwaters have not receded but have simply changed position. Any depth contour map of the oceans will show the land masses that existed before the Flood. But it is the discovery of so many animal species at the same time, their bones broken and fused together in great piles as the waters swirled them around within caverns and crevasses, that furnish perhaps the most convincing evidence of the Flood and destruction that changed the earth.

There is, of course, another element pertinent to mankind's intuitive memory of the Flood. This would be the finding of a ship on Mount Ararat.

10

The Clash of Ideas

A personal announcement appeared in the *London Daily Telegraph* of May 12, 1967. It reads as follows:

> URGENTLY NEED name date or any information regarding elderly man who died between 1917 and 1925 and who confessed on death bed that in his youth he had climbed Mount Ararat and found Noah's Ark Write U.N. 1725 Daily Telegraph IC.

This insertion appears to have a connection with the frequently quoted report concerning a reputed visit to the Ark in the 1850s by five people, three British scientist-explorers and two Armenian guides, father and son. This unusual incident has been quoted by a number of Ark researchers but most completely researched in a book by Violet Cummings *(Has Anyone Really Seen Noah's Ark?)*, assisted by her daughter, Phyllis Watson Cummings and by her husband, Eryl Cummings. (An entire family dedicated to the search for the Ark!) Eryl Cummings, who has made eighteen ascents of Ararat, has compiled a file of Ark research now measuring fifty feet in length, probably the most complete Ark file extant.

147

The above-quoted mid-nineteenth-century sighting, having to do with sworn secrecy, deathbed confessions, and remarkable coincidences (of which the previously quoted personal item is but one example) is considered by the Cummings and other researchers as a pertinent proof that a number of reliable witnesses have seen the Ark. It is also illustrative of the clash between religious belief and the scorn of skeptics, the ongoing clash between those who hold the Bible to be history and the scientific community, including a number of Biblical experts, who do not.

Scientific criticism of what seems to be scientifically impossible in the Biblical account of Creation, the Ark, the Flood, and the ensuing early history of man, has existed among "freethinkers" throughout the Middle Ages although, due to the presence of a number of inhibiting factors, such as the possibility of being burned at the stake, dissenting opinions were kept as private as possible. During the era of revolutionary thought, starting in France with Voltaire and the Encyclopedists, attacks were initiated on the traditional beliefs of the Old and New Testaments. Less than a hundred years later the Darwinian theory of evolution brought into doubt the Biblical creation of man, a problem still under discussion as new discoveries in Africa and elsewhere seem to establish man's appearance on the planet first as hundreds of thousands of years ago and then further extended to several million years.

During this war of ideas initiated or at least popularized by Darwin, a number of atheist or Darwinian clubs were formed in England. Coincidentally, at about this time, reports started coming out of Asia Minor through Turkish sources about the rediscovery of the Ark as the result of seismic activity on Mount Ararat.

With this news it occurred to several independently wealthy members of one of these English scientific clubs that it would be something of a lark to go to Turkey, climb Mount Ararat, and establish that the reported discovery of the Ark was false.

The three friends arrived in Bayazit (now Doğubayazit) in the early 1850s and came in contact with an Armenian guide who informed them that he could guide them to Noah's Ark. They engaged him but their investigation on the mountain did not have the result they expected. The guide's son, named Yearam, eventually came to America and survived until 1920. Yearam's account is the only firsthand report to come down through the years, except a somewhat shadowy near "deathbed" confession apparently from one of the English skeptics.

Yearam, almost sixty-five years after his trip up Mount Ararat with his father and the Englishmen, dictated his memories of what had happened to Harold and Ida Williams, his benefactors and hosts in California. Yearam, now called Haji (the pilgrim) Yearam because of a pilgrimage he had made to Jerusalem, was now old and ill and, in his opinion, near death. He told his hosts that he wished to make an important statement before he died. He had never told anyone his secret as he had sworn an oath never to reveal it but now, since he was about to die and as the others concerned had probably already died, it no longer mattered.

His secret was about Noah's Ark. He said that his father had guided the English expedition up the mountain and had found the Ark without much difficulty as considerable melting had taken place. It was located partly in the glacier whose melting had made a lake nearby. It was possible to climb up the side of the Ark and to ascertain that it was a vessel with a superstructure of several levels and seeming to correspond in measurements with the fabled Ark. However, instead of showing satisfaction at the unusual find, the English scientists were furious at being proved wrong and extracted sworn oaths, under penalty of death, from Yearam and his father never to mention the find to anyone. Yearam, although he spent long years in America, far from Ararat, never did betray his oath until he felt that he himself was about to die. The details were written down in a notebook, signed by Yearam and witnessed by Harold and Ida Williams. Yearam, despite his vision of approaching death, did not die until five years later, in 1920.

Some time after Yearam's death Williams read a short article in his hometown newspaper, from Brockton, Massachusetts, concerning an English scientist who, before his death, confessed to his family that he was one of the explorers who had visited the Ark and had terrified the Armenians into swearing never to mention the discovery. As for himself, he and his two associates had simply made a "gentlemen's pact" never to divulge what they had done or what they had discovered.

The notebook signed by Yearam and the news item from Brockton both burned in a butane gas explosion in 1940 in the Williams' later school-sanitorium in Louisiana. In addition, however, to the Cummings archives and statements from the Williamses and other people who knew Haji Yearam, there remains still the 1967 "personal" from the *London Daily Telegraph*—an apparent request for information about Yearam from a source that is now untraceable.

Eryl Cummings is an example of a searcher for the

Ark whose compelling interest in establishing the Ark's existence has extended over his entire life, ever since he first heard about the Ark in Sunday school when he was four or five years old. This early impression which influenced his whole life is reminiscent of that of Heinrich Schliemann, the discoverer of ancient Troy, who was impelled in his career of archaeological exploration and the finding of Troy by the memory of a historical poster showing the great walls of Troy which he saw at the age of seven. Cummings used the income from a successful business career to finance seventeen personal expeditions to Ararat, thus following in the footsteps of Schliemann and Fernand Navarra. He made his last trip in 1986, undaunted at the age of eighty-two. He has been badly injured on the mountain by being thrown by fractious horses, an accident causing him not to interrupt his search on the mountain but to modify his choice of mounts to the less temperamental mule or ass.

Sometimes discoveries, previously held back for many years, unexpectedly surface. Cummings believes he has recently made contact with a reliable firsthand witness who has seen the Ark, but he is not yet ready to reveal names or locations, principally because of pressures on such an individual from other searchers and even possible dangers as implied by the case of George Jefferson Greene (page 47). The person involved claims to have found the Ark forty-one years ago, in the general area (above Ahora Gorge) where Cummings and a number of others believe it to be located. He says he found it during a period of favorable melting and that his guides had entered the interior of the wooden ship while he himself was unable to because of sudden bad weather. He claims, however, that he saw the wooden mass from across another icy ridge. The guides allegedly found foodstuffs frozen inside the vessel and gave some of them to the explorer—seeds, honey, and lentils. It is to be hoped that these frozen provisions might eventually be tested for age to ascertain whether they are in the earliest time frame of the pieces of wood found by Navarra on the mountains. Wheat has been dated from Egyptian tombs of Pharaonic times and divers have drunk wine obtained from still stoppered amphorae which they had brought up from ancient shipwrecks on the bottom of the Mediterranean. But the wine, according to their reports, had definitely not improved with age.

Eryl Cummings and the other dedicated explorers who go back to Ararat every year in their search for the Ark are examples of those whose faith in the Bible leads them to consider that the events described therein are factual history. This opinion is rarely shared by scientists. The scientific-archaeological point of view has been succinctly expressed by Dr. Frolich Rainey, who was director of the University Museum at the University of Pennsylvania at the time that Navarra's pieces of wood were given a carbon-14 rating of only A.D. 560—a time hardly compatible with the Flood legend. In Dr. Rainey's opinion: "Absolutely anything is possible in this world, but if there's anything that's impossible in archaeology—this is it."

But despite the generally unfriendly scientific opinion about the factual value of the Old Testament, it should be noted that geographical and terrain information contained in the Old Testament was of considerable value to British staff officers in military operations in Palestine, Jordan, and Syria during World War I, an indication that familiarity with the Bible has unexpected advantages. As Egerton Sykes observed some years ago,

"More material regarding the Old Testament has turned up in the last thirty years than in the previous 2000 . . . the story of the Ark should not, therefore, be [summarily] dismissed. . . ."

While it is understandable that convinced free-thinkers would have been strenuously opposed to the close interpretation of Genesis establishing the physical presence of the Ark in the "mountains of Ararat" it is nevertheless surprising to find that there are a number of religious authorities on Biblical studies who consider that a belief in the Ark legend is no longer tenable in the light of what is now known about the facts of ancient history. Some, like Father David Maria Turoldo, an Italian theologian quoted by Mario Zanot in *Dopo il Diluvio,* suggest that a great flood did take place but affected Mesopotamia and contiguous parts of the Middle East which, at that time and place, *did* seem to the survivors to encompass "the world." In past ages there have always been survivors of great natural catastrophes. Such individuals are described, as was Noah, as just and righteous men. This quality of righteousness applied to them by later generations is in itself a justification as to why certain individuals were saved. Father Turoldo suggests that even after a possible modern world-catastrophe—such as unrestricted atomic warfare—there will still be some survivors, new Noahs saved by chance or design to live on and perpetuate the human race.

Other Biblical authorities such as Dr. Howard Teeple, executive director of the Religion and Ethics Institute of Evanston, Illinois, take the view that belief in the Ark legend is not only erroneous but misleading. Referring to the Ark legend Dr. Teeple has stated: "With my professional training in ancient history and Biblical scholarship I know that Noah's Ark is not on Mount

Ararat because Noah's Ark never existed in the first place." In his book *The Noah's Ark Nonsense* Dr. Teeple has traced how the Sumerian-Babylonian legend was adopted by Judaism and Christianity and spread over the world in ever widening waves as an attractive story without, however, any historical or geological foundation. (But this theory would not explain the Flood legends prevalent throughout Asia, Europe, Africa, the Americas, and the Pacific islands thousands of years prior to European penetration of these areas.)

In 1977 Dr. Teeple saw, in the *Chicago Daily News*, an advertisement for a television special movie *In Search of Noah's Ark* adapted from a book of the same name written by Dave Balsiger and Charles Sellier, Jr., and published in 1976. Dr. Teeple related that ". . . with pencil and paper in hand I monitored the telecast. The film was even worse than I had feared." He objected especially to the film's attempt "to persuade the audience that the Ark is there [on Mount Ararat] and also that the Bible as a whole is literally true." He observed that "The film did not mention the fact that its thesis [the Flood and Mount Ararat] has long been rejected by the seminaries of mainline churches and by the religion and history departments of nearly all colleges and universities in the western world."

Dr. Teeple thereupon wrote a letter of protest to NBC charging them with irresponsible broadcasting and sent a copy to the FCC in Washington. Dr. Teeple in his protest to NBC requested that a nationwide prime-time show be filmed and telecast presenting what would essentially be an anti-Ark production to maintain the channel's reputation for fairness. Dr. Teeple claimed that the film was sectarian propaganda "for it tries to show . . . in fundamentalist fashion that the Bible is true" and protested against the film's "unfairness to scientists and to genuine historians, archaeologists, and Biblical scholars."

NBC eventually replied, stating that the program had been presented "only as entertainment" while the FCC stated that the program did not discuss a controversial issue of public importance and by inference did not need a reply. To this Dr. Teeple replies, considering the fundamentalist vs. the historical approach to the Bible has caused the "break between the Bible schools and the main [religious] seminaries. If this issue is not controversial—what is?"

Pertinent scientific comments about the Ark and the Flood have been voiced by Dr. Bulent Atalay, a physics professor at Mary Washington College in Fredericksburg, Virginia. As reported in *Pursuit,* a magazine published by the Society for the Investigation of the Unexplained, based on a news report. Dr. Atalay has special qualifications as a commentator on the Ark; he is Turkish, the son of a Turkish general, familiar with the terrain through personal visits and capable of considering the Flood and the Ark from a scientific point of view.

Dr. Atalay has examined the wood brought back from Ararat by Navarra, the piece carbon-dated as being 4000 to 5000 years old. He agrees that there are adz marks hewn on the wood, showing that it was hand formed. He thinks that the wood may have come from some old shrine or other construction built on Mount Ararat by peoples of the far past such as Hittites, Hurrians, Babylonians, or Sumerians and now frozen under the ice.

As a scientist he thinks that the report of the Ark's present existence at a high altitude of 13,000 to 14,000 feet and the possibility that it landed on an even higher altitude such as 17,000 feet is difficult to believe. He says: "There's no way I can accept water rising to 17,000 feet. . . . There simply is not enough water in the atmosphere if you were to condense it at the Poles or even if you were to melt them, to get [a worldwide depth] above three or four hundred meters."*

In 1984 Dr. Atalay accompanied Marvin Steffins, the president of International Expeditions, to the Ark form eighteen miles from Mount Ararat, which he describes as "having the shape of an enormous pistachio" but also decided that "it looks like a ship." He adds: "The dimensions are just about what the Bible suggests as the size of the Ark—three hundred cubits long." The fact that the altitude of the shiplike object is 5000 feet instead of 15,000 feet "is certainly a bit more palatable." Noting that the object is not on Mount Ararat but a considerable distance from it, across a valley and then up another range of hills, causes him to think that it may have been left there by a serious local flood. After it was beached, he suggests, a fortification was perhaps built around it and therefore it is difficult to dig through the

---

*As an example of unexpected scientific substantiation of the frequently voiced fundamentalist theory that Flood waters came from outside the earth in a great cosmic cloud containing water, Louis Frank, a University of Iowa physicist, who is supported in this theory by other scientists from the University of Iowa, claims that at some time in the past this may have happened. According to an article in *The New York Times*, April 1986, Dr. Frank suggests that the water in the earth's oceans was not always here in its present quantity but, coming from the solar system, caused the ice sheets and an increased layer in the atmosphere. He points out that the presence of water eruptions on the moon, water vapor in the atmosphere of Venus, dark areas in the rings of Saturn, and icy cliffs on the moons of Uranus, for example, indicate the presence of water in cosmic space. Although this theory has been postulated to apply to an extremely remote era, it is still an interesting example of frequent similarity between legendary beliefs and scientific theory.

shape in order to get datable material. Atalay has a certain familiarity with the Ark on Mount Ararat legend since his uncle, the director of the Archaeological Museum in Istanbul, had gone to Ararat in the 1950s to ascertain "once and for all whether there was anything up there." As far as the Flood itself was concerned Dr. Atalay observes, "There is not enough water on the earth now and there would not have been 5000 years ago to actually submerge most of the earth."

David Fasold, previously referred to in Chapter 4, is among the more positive and vocal adherents of the theory of the Ark form of the above 1984 expedition being Noah's Ark. He was interviewed by the author on his return from the Ararat area in 1985.

Question: What do you consider the most convincing proof of the shiplike formation at Tendürek being the Ark?

In the first place Tendürek is the wrong name, a mistake followed by all writers about the Ark. The formation is located in the Akyayla Range where anyone who goes there can see it. It is located at latitude 39° 26.4″ N and longitude 44° 15.3″ E and is 11.3 kilometers southeast of Doğubayazit. The altitude of its north and south ends above sea level is 6240 and 6250 feet respectively. But if you ask for proof I say it is the thirteen longitudinal lines shown by subsurface radar on which you get an iron reading every thirty to forty centimeters, and the nine transverse bulkheads. Remember that the Babylonian description of the Ark described it as having *nine* divisions.

What do you consider the other ships found on Ararat to be?

When you are talking about ships on Ararat you are really talking about a collection of them. Roskovitsky said he saw one shaped like a submarine with a whaleback bearing three stubby masts with just enough sail to turn it into the wind. George Hagopian described the Ark as being a thousand feet long and six hundred feet wide. Prince Nouri said what he visited was three hundred yards long. Reports go from rectangular boxes to submarines; tradition says that a willow tree sprang up from one of the Ark's planks.

Would any of the reported discoveries of the Ark correspond with the buried Ark?

Reşit's discovery in 1948 would. He said that he saw the inward-curving lines of a ship in his fields, which has now been further exposed through erosion and also seismic movement has dropped the level of the ground so that the object is now more noticeable. Remember that Resit said: "It is not a rock formation. I know a ship when I see one." The clue in Reşit's story is that he said that the villagers who came to see it went away in surprise since there was no tradition about the Ark being there. In other words it was not on Ararat. The reason Reşit was never found was because people were looking for him in the villages of Ararat twenty miles away while the real Reşit was living to the south, probably waiting for someone to come and interview him. On June 24, 1986, a man named Reşit was located and interviewed by David Fasold through the simple expedient of going to Mahşer, now known as Uzengili, and asking if a man named

Reşit lived there. He did, and he was willing to talk about the buried Ark. His full name was Reşit Sarihan and he stated that he was the same Reşit whose story of finding the Ark appeared in the Istanbul press in 1948, at which time he was twenty years old. He stated that an earthquake which occurred in the middle of May of that year had forced up the shiplike shape from beneath the earth in a field that Reşit was renting. He said, "It came up in the middle of my field and ruined it! Some of the village inhabitants interpreted the appearance of the Ark as a bad omen and the people of twenty houses moved away." It was some time after this that the original name of the village, Mahşer—"Doomsday" was changed to Uzengili—"Stirrup."

Do you think that the Ark shape now at Akyayla was once higher up on Mount Ararat? Is there any visible indication of where it was formerly located?

It never was on Ararat. It landed in a high valley to the east and later slid down about a thousand feet to where it now is. It followed an alluvial flow when it slid down but was stopped by a large rock which broke into its side and rotated it to its present position. The break in its port bulwark can still be seen. The rock ledge held it there and it got covered by mud coming down the mountain. I think the bowstem is still a thousand feet higher up, where the Ark first landed and where the stone anchors can still be seen.

* * *

Considering the size of the Ark do you think that eight people could have sailed the vessel and taken care of all the animals?

I would think that more than eight were aboard. Noah and Shem were what we would now call the prime contractors. A ship of that size was probably built in a year through the efforts of a number of people, some of whom probably sailed with Noah on the Ark.

If this is the Ark, what happened to the wood?

The word "gopherwood" used in Genesis is certainly an error in translation. The word appears no place else in the Bible. What we have here is a reed boat covered by a bituminous substance such as asphalt with pumice and other catalytic agents, followed by pitch—in other words basically a cement vessel. That is why it seems to be made of stone. The only pumice you have in the immediate area is in the shape of this boat. There are manganese modules coming out of the Ark, decomposed feldspar and calcium silicate—all part of a bituminous conglomeration poured over a reed framework.

Would such a ship float?

Do cement ships float? Of course they do! Iron ships float and cement ships float. Even during World War I we constructed cement ships called "The Kaiser's Coffins" and in World War II we built whole fleets of cement ships.

How do you correlate the Biblical measurements given for the Ark with the measurements of the ship at Akyayla?

There is a variety of cubits. The cubit the Bible refers to in this case is the same cubit used in the Great Pyramid of Pharaoh Khufu and the Pillars of Solomon's Temple—that is 20.6 inches. As the vessel we have here measures 515 feet we get *exact* results if we multiply the 20.6 cubit by 300 [300 × 20.6 = 6180, and 6180 ÷ 12 = 515].

Do you think that the Akyayla formation will ever be accepted as Noah's Ark?

I think that archaeologists will accept it, especially when the interior is photographed by interface radar, as a great survival ship of Sumerian times. The contours still show the upswept bow and stern similar to representations of ships of ancient Mesopotamia and the papyrus boats of Egypt. But I don't think fundamentalists will accept it as they seem to think that if it is not on Ararat and of *rectangular* shape it is not the Ark. Anyway, the idea of the Ark being rectangular comes from a mistake in translating the Bible into Greek, when the word for "Ark"—the Hebrew *tabah* was translated into Greek as *kibotos,* meaning "box." Also, the Bible never said the Ark was on Mount Ararat but *in the mountains of Ararat* [Armenia]. That is why when almost everybody is looking for it on Ararat a few others are in search of Noah's Ark wherever we can find it.

An ingenious explanation tying in the Ark shape with the landing of the Ark on Mount Ararat has been offered by Egerton Sykes: "My own reconstruction of the sequence of events is that the Ark did actually land on or near Ararat at a time when the flanks of the mountain were covered with semiliquid lava into which the vessel sank leaving the now famous impression. There is no reason why timbers should not have remained *in situ* for thousands of years until they were removed for housebuilding or even as fuel by the local farmers."

Sykes predicted, from personal experience, probable Russian reticence to allow foreign examination of alleged timbers from the Ark: "It is extremely doubtful

Reconstruction of the "buried" Ark in the Akyayla range showing the basic construction features. The flow lines in the terrain under the presumed ship indicate its descent from a higher level. The opening in the side is an indication of where it was caught on a rock formation in its descent. The artist now feels, in the light of subsequent discoveries, that the ship was not covered with planking but with a form of cement applied over reed mats. *Drawing © David Fasold*

whether the Soviets would cooperate by allowing the reputed timber from the Ark in Echmiadzin Cathedral to be examined by independent experts, as the verification of the existence of Noah and of his Ark might be assumed to be running contrary to their religious policy."

The considerable distance (seventeen miles between Ararat and the formation on the Akyayla Range seems definitely to preclude the probability of the two sites representing remnants of the same ship. Therefore we are left with the intriguing possibility of there being *two* ancient ships (or Arks) in the same area; one on Mount Ararat and the other on the Akyayla Range next to the village with the strange name of Mahser (Doomsday). The question of which is the real Ark is further compounded by the statement in the Koran, the Holy Book of Islam, that the Ark landed on the mountain Al Judi. The Koran, containing as it does a great deal of material in common with the Old Testament and some parts of the New Testament, definitely states in Sura XI *(Hud)* when describing the end of the Flood: ". . . And it was said O earth swallow up thy waters, and thou O heaven, withhold thy rain." And immediately the water abated and the decree was fulfilled, and the Ark rested on the Mountain of Judi. . . ."

Mount Al Judi, spelled Cudi-Dağh in Turkish means "highest" or "the heights" in Arabic and for this reason a number of people in Eastern Turkey, including some Islamic scholars, think *Al Judi* refers to *Ararat.* But Cudi-Dağh is actually located south of Lake Van, rising to a height of 7700 feet. The local tribesmen there maintain that the Ark drifted to a high point in the Cudi mountain chain and that the remains of it are still on the top of Cudi-Dağh, the highest mountain in that area. A

German writer-mountaineer, F. Bender, described in an article in *Kosmos* (published in Stuttgart) how he and a Kurdish party in 1956 climbed to the top of Cudi-Dağh and "found wooden remains on the peak."

In addition to the above peaks there is another Al Judi still further to the south near the Turko-Syrian border. In Iran, Mount Demavend is commonly supposed to be the resting place of the Ark with remnants of it still near the summit. The late Ivan Sanderson, author, explorer, former British intelligence officer, and founder of the Society for the Investigation of the Unexplained, has commented, in his own investigation of the Ark, on the "variety of 'Arks' strewn around the Turko-Russian-Iraqi-Iranian frontiers."

Among the newspaper stories originating from the reported discovery of two or more Arks, the *London Daily Telegraph* commented on ". . . the discovery of two Arks . . . one in North Anatolia and the other miles away near the Syrian border . . ." then added, in a burst of restrained British humor, "Like everything else in the story of Noah it seems right that Arks should come in twos as well."

But the mountains where the survival ships reputedly landed, according to the multiple legends passed on by tribes and peoples throughout the world, are not limited to two any more than are the Arks. The mountains also extend over the entire world. Some are identifiable, while others appear to be legendary or may have had their names changed since antiquity. Still others are man-made mountains such as the pyramid of Cholula in Mexico and the pyramid of Khufu in Egypt, which were reputedly constructed to safeguard man's accumulated knowledge (Khufu) or to provide a refuge (Cholula) from a universal flood.

The mountains mentioned in the Flood legends are at least fifty and the legends of certain individuals or tribal leaders who escaped a catastrophic flood and started life again in a changed world are more than a hundred.

The survival of mankind menaced by a flood through the agency of a providential ship that will save it from the waters is a natural and feasible idea, the first narrative in Genesis that needs no theological reasoning to be understood. This concept has been preserved by all peoples through written records, drawings, and stone carvings since the era of pre-history. Deep within the caves of Europe, Africa, Asia, and the Americas one finds an unusual preoccupation with the representation of large boats, capable of carrying many people, incised on the cavern walls, along with other simpler pictures of mammoths, aurochs, wild horses, and other edible animals as well as those more dangerous to primitive hunters. But these cave drawings of boats, sometimes carrying animals and always crowded with people, are the only pictorial representations of groups of men (other than some simple hunting scenes) found on cave walls from the times of prehistoric man. These boats, whether found in early Sumeria, Egypt, Spain, Switzerland, Great Britain, Scandinavia, Northwest Africa, or California, bear a startling resemblance to each other, and certain individuals on these craft seem to be carrying the same standards, resembling a sunburst. If these boats are a remembrance of a mass flight from a flood then these navigators were survivors other than the Noahs of the Middle East, and the concept of a catastrophic flood affecting the entire world becomes an understandable reality.

The artifact allegedly so often glimpsed on Mount

Ararat could have survived for many centuries if covered by glacial ice. Wood, a material generally quickly decayed, will survive under ice, frozen mud, muck, earth, or sand. Mud is an excellent preserver of tissue, human or animal, as has been shown in the saber-toothed tigers found in Alaska and Northern Canada, mammoths in Siberia, and even certain human corpses, thousands of years old, found deep in mud deposits in Denmark, Poland, and England, the only corpses among the uncounted billions of the earth's dead whose faces have preserved the exact features their owners had in life a hundred centuries ago. Sand, earth, and ice have revealed the existence of other great ships through the centuries, ships whose form, decorations, and sometimes written inscriptions resemble no known maritime cultures.

Such a ship was found near Naples at the end of the fifteenth century and was described by Giovanni Pontaro, an Italian historian who visited the site (Harold Wilkins: *Secret Cities of South America*). The vessel was found as a result of a seismic disturbance splitting the top of a mountain, when a very ancient ship burst out of the mountain amidst great boulders and avalanches of stones and earth. Examination indicated that the wreck was quite different from other ancient ships of the Mediterranean, being neither Roman, Greek, Carthaginian, or Phoenician, and that it was so old that it was petrified.

The above allusion to petrification reminds one of the buried "Ark" at Akyayla, south of Doğubayazit, whose apparent gunwales seemed to be made of stone, solid earth, or cement. It is also reminiscent of the lava casts of human figures and even of dogs at Pompeii and Herculaneum, casts which have effectively immortalized some of the victims of the lava flow from Mount Vesuvius in A.D. 79.

Another such incident took place in Switzerland, also in the fifteenth century. Miners, digging in a shaft 100 feet below the surface, found a large iron anchor and then the remains of a wooden ship "well fashioned," decorated with carvings and still holding numerous human skulls within its broken timbers. In 1540, only a few years after the conquest of Peru, Spanish gold hunters searching for hidden treasures of gold and silver and mines which they thought the Peruvian Indians were still keeping secret encountered a wooden wall in a passage they were digging under a hill near Callao. Further digging revealed the remains of a large wooden ship quite unlike the seagoing ships which the Incas used in their ocean trips off the western coast of South America.

Another mysterious ancient ship was found during the Alaskan gold rush and described in some detail in the *San Francisco Examiner,* June 1908, which reported the find of a "hull of a great ship high up on the hills within the Arctic Circle and far to the interior from the sea." The discovery was made by a miner, M. J. Brown, who corroborated reports previously made by K. C. Moran and other miners, Alaskan natives, and Russians. Brown stated to the press that the vessel was of "enormous proportions" and had evidently been used for some time by the Indians as "a place in which to dry salmon." It was suggested that the large structure was not a ship but a floating Russian fort (!) which had been washed up many miles inland, but further examination emphasized the shape of a ship 300 feet long, with entries, apertures, and passageways. The frozen wood appeared to be of great age and was characterized by unusual decorations and inscriptions. The writing used in the inscriptions, according to those who saw it and were familiar with several languages, was neither Russian, Chinese, Greek, nor any other modern language known to the viewers.

One cannot assess how many other ships still lie under the earth or under the sea bottom since, if they were on the sea bottom, they would probably long since have disappeared. Ships that have been found buried under hills probably got there when their pilots were fleeing from a catastrophic flood which produced such tremendous waves that the vessels were not only washed up on land but, through the action of successive waves and the force of the floodwaters, they were literally buried under the mud which later hardened over them. There they remained for thousands of years until miners found them. The miners, unconcerned with any possible value to themselves or to archaeology, which at that time was a science yet to come, used the timbers to shore up the mineshaft and therefore destroyed the evidence.

Villagers living in the French Alps near Chambéry used to show travelers huge iron and brass rings fixed solidly into rocks in the mountains, the purpose of which was not apparent. The explanation given by the villagers for these mysterious rings was that they were mooring rings for vessels "in the days when the Deluge covered the land. . . ." Large stone anchors, part of the equipment of the ships of antiquity, were formed by great rectangular, triangular, or teardrop-shaped stones perforated at the top so that chains or ropes could be passed through the holes.

Two such anchors near Mount Ararat were examined by Ron Wyatt during a 1978 expedition. He determined that they were anchor stones because of their shape and the round opening cut at the top. The stones are still lying on a plain on low hills about seven miles southwest of Doğubayazit. They are ten feet high, five feet wide, and two feet thick at the bottom. They may have originally belonged to either the Ark under the glacier or to the buried or silicated Ark at Mahşer or even to a still different vessel. The two anchors, of which one is split at the hole, seem to lie in a line with the buried Ark's theoretical slide down the mountain. They are not conglomerates but are made of solid stone. The anchors have been incised with eight crosses, purportedly signifying the eight persons on the Ark of Noah, crosses probably carved by Armenians or other Christian pilgrims after the anchors were first discovered hundreds or thousands of years ago.

Whatever the origin of these crosses, it is the anchors themselves that suggest a pertinent question: If the Mahşer "Ark" is merely a natural formation and the Ararat vessel simply an ancient wooden building or fort, why are these great ship anchors on the slope of Mount Ararat?

11

The Ark and Reality

The physical cause of the Great Flood has been ascribed by those scientists who believe in it to a variety of geological and/or astronomical happenings, none of which, with the exception of the melting of the last glaciation, has been conclusively proved. These theories include: the intrusion of a planet (Venus) within our solar system with the ensuing chaos on the planet earth; the capture by earth of a smaller planet (now the moon); the passing of earth through the tail of a comet or the head-on collision with the comet's head; a sudden collision between earth and a large asteroid, sinking islands into the ocean and causing tidal waves over the earth; a polar shift and/or a change in the earth's rotation accompanied by considerable land-sea changes and enormous temporary floods.

These are the scientific explanations of geology, astronomy, and climatology. Many scientists, perhaps the majority, are opposed to a concept of a flood rolling over the earth's surface with cosmic waves breaking high against its mountains and prefer a more gradual and cadenced explanation: changes in animal species and the shape of the land have come gradually. Nothing especially violent, it is postulated, except earthquakes, has happened for hundreds of thousands, perhaps millions, of years. In contrast to this theory of gradual change it must be observed that, with the finds of the last century, the pendulum of scientific thought has tended to swing away from the comfortable theory of gradual change to a more dramatic picture—from the relatively sudden termination of the great dinosaurs (after a planetary rule of 55,000,000 years) to the extinction of many of the earth's larger mammals in the relatively modern era of 11,000 to 12,000 years before present.

Besides the scientific explanations and sometimes combined with them there are religious traditions, held throughout the centuries and still believed in in varying degrees by a large part of the earth's population. These beliefs coincide in the matter of a flood and tidal waves, often accompanied by earthquakes, volcanic eruptions, and the sinking and sometimes rising of extensive land areas. Understandably the flood legends of the world's races consider the catastrophe to be due to man's having offended God, heaven, or particular gods of the Babylonian, Sumerian, or Egyptian religious pantheons.

Judeo-Christian-Islamic traditions imply that mankind was punished for its evil actions with a few exceptions being made for exemplary individuals, such as Noah and his family. Mankind was simply washed out of existence to enable humanity to start anew. In effect a Divine warning was given to mankind through Noah's construction of the Ark, but man neglected to observe it.

What was mankind doing to incur the wrath of God? The Old Testament provides only general information. Genesis 6:5: "And God saw that the wickedness

of man was great in the earth, and that every imagination of the thoughts of his heart was only evil continually," and 6:11: "The earth also was corrupt before
God, and the earth was filled with violence."

Later references to man's punishment contained in
the New Testament relate Divine punishment to the life-
style of Sodom and Gomorrah: 2 Peter 2:5 and 6, "And
spared not the old world, but saved Noah . . . a
preacher of righteousness, bringing in the flood upon
the world of the ungodly; And turning the cities of
Sodom and Gomorrah into ashes . . . making them an
example unto those that after them should live ungodly."

The Koran also says that Noah was given the opportunity of warning the people of Ad that the Flood
was coming. (It is interesting to note that Ad or At is the
first syllable of Atlantis in a number of ancient cultures.)
In Sura VII of the Koran it is written: "The leaders of
his people said 'We see thee evidently wandering [in
mind].'" And again: "Ah, we see thou art an imbecile
and we think thou art a liar." To which Noah replied, "I
am not an imbecile but an apostle from the Lord and
Cherisher of the worlds. I but fulfill toward you the
duties of my Lord's mission." The implication of this is
that God was giving the people of Ad a chance to re-
form their lives and survive.

Sura VII tells of the outcome: "Noah's warning was
rejected by his generation and they were destroyed in
the Flood. Hud [another prophet] was defied by his own
people [the] Ad," but they were swept away by a terrific
blast. Their successors, the Thamud, were puffed up
with pride and injustice—but behold, "An earthquake
buried them for their sins. . . . With a rain of brimstone
and fire were overwhelmed the Cities of the Plain for

their unexampled lusts, against which Lot did warn them."

The reference to Lot and the destroyed cities, coupled and apparently connected with references to the Flood and Noah also occurs in the New Testament (2 Peter 2:5-6 and Luke 17:26-29). It causes one to wonder whether Sodom and Gomorrah were victims of seismic disasters which occurred at the time of the Flood.

In the world's many legends a number of different reasons have been given for heaven's displeasure. Certainly one of the most unusual is that of the punishment of mankind by some of the gods of the Babylonian legends who thought that man was making too much noise and disturbing the gods in their heaven, perhaps the earliest mention of noise pollution. In Amerindian legends there are references to the punishment of heaven over the killing of certain sacred animals or the breaking of other taboos. This guilt of an individual or of a tribe for the violating of taboos is found in groups from the Arctic to the end of South America and the Pacific islands and, in legend, has been the cause of heavenly punishment by flood, earthquake, and fire. Other ancient commentators have suggested that great catastrophes come in circular patterns independent of man's actions for good or evil. Heraclitus, the Greek philosopher, consulting ancient records and legends, thought that global catastrophes occurred every 10,000 to 11,000 years. As the last glacial change happened 11,000 years ago, the next world catastrophe, at least according to Heraclitus' theory, is due in the fairly near future.

Among the variety of reasons either attributed to heavenly powers or to natural causes for the almost annihilation of the human race at the time of the Flood there are certain memories and written traditions from ancient cultures such as Egypt, Greece, India, and even from Indian tribes in America, that suggest that the catastrophe was brought on by man himself through the use of destructive forces which got out of control. This has been suggested in the writings of Plato and others who relate them to the doom of Atlantis, once the center of a powerful empire in the Atlantic Ocean, which perished in a fatal final war. The concept of unlimited warfare causing the end of a former world has been preserved in the legends of the Hopi Indians, now a small remnant of a once more numerous people, a war that took place so long ago that accounts of it are lost in time with the exception of certain memories handed down from generation to generation from the distant past.

These recollections (*Book of the Hopi*: Frank Waters/White Bear) tell of great cities and civilizations on the earth that ended because "when people had what they wanted, they wanted more still and wars began . . . ," culminating in the destruction of the great cities by *patuwvotas* (superbombers) in wars which ceased only when the land and sea had changed places, leaving on the sea bottom "all the proud cities, the flying patuwvotas, and worldly treasures corrupted with evil. . . ."

It is in the Hindu classics, notably in the *Mahabharata*, that the most startling descriptions of prehistoric warfare and its effects have been written. These refer to events that happened thousands of years before the *Mahabharata* was written, remembering that this classic was written in antiquity. The events described were considered fanciful accounts of warfare between the gods when the *Mahabharata* was first translated into

175

European languages beginning in the 1830s. At that time they made no sense to the reader. At the present time, however, after two World Wars and subsequent events, their strange references are easily understandable.

Sections of the *Mahabharata,* such as the *Mausala Parva* and the *Drona Parva* describe a bomb ("The Iron Thunderbolt of Death") which exploded "with the brightness of ten thousand suns" and which was capable of killing many thousands of the enemy with one explosion. Its burst was characterized by billowing death clouds spreading upward and opening like "giant parasols," sucking upward into its center soldiers, chariots, horses, and elephants and leaving burned and unrecognizable corpses. The wounded who survived were horribly burned; they lost parts of their skin, their hair and nails fell out, and they later died. Even the contamination of food was described as well as the need for the survivors to wash themselves and their equipment in flowing streams. As a final coincidence the measurement of such an "Iron Thunderbolt"—three cubits plus six feet—is the same size as the second atomic bomb used in combat—the one dropped on Nagasaki. All of us have known since 1945 that our bombs were real and final. But were the destructive bombs of ancient India, so completely described, only the dreams of scribes?

In answer to the above question one might observe that numerous skeletons found in excavated streets of Mohenjo-daro, located in Pakistan, were found to be the most radioactive human or animal remains ever found.

The Old Testament in Zechariah 14:12 gives a startling description of casualties in a future conflict which closely resembles that given in the *Mahabharata:* ". . . Their flesh shall consume away while they stand

176

upon their feet, and their eyes shall consume away in their holes. . . ."

Another forecast (or memory?) of what we now can associate with a description of atomic war is found in the Book of Esdras (the Biblical Apocrypha): ". . . great and mighty clouds . . . shall arise to destroy the earth and its inhabitants . . . no one will be left to cultivate the earth or to sow it. . . ."

The persuasive references in the *Mahabharata* of what we now recognize as perceptive descriptions of the use of atomic bombs in warfare calls into question the possibility of the discovery and use of atomic energy by a civilization which existed before what we now recognize as history. However, since our own culture has attained an atomic capability in a space of six thousand years, and man's civilized existence is being constantly pushed further back in time by new archaeological discoveries, humanity may be considered to have had ten or fifteen times that time space to develop a whole series of civilizations which were destroyed or destroyed themselves through atomic or man-made catastrophes.

The consistent threat of sudden annihilation with a preliminary warning (if given at all) of only minutes has conditioned people all over the world to expect this "worst case" which the proliferation of atomic warheads and the increasing number of quarrelsome national entities that are now making their own bombs does little to assuage.

One should note from history that all weapons that have been invented have been used, and more than once. The effects of thermonuclear warfare, whether launched on earth, in space, or from space, imply the possible end of the world—at least for humanity. This ending might be a sudden one if quantities of nuclear warheads explode in sufficient force to change the angle of the earth's rotation, to melt the icecaps, to turn the atmosphere into poisonous vapor, or to blow a hole in the protective ozone layer surrounding the planet. A more gradual and perhaps more painful finish would result from an "atomic winter" and the death of herds and elimination of food crops, either as a result of atmospheric or temperature modification or the effects of radiation, and man, like the dinosaurs, would disappear from the planet.

Realization of what we are faced with has provoked public interest in prophecies of the present, and also from the past, affecting our future. This interest is notable even among groups most well informed about the progress of science, an anachronism that, one would think, should be properly relegated to the superstitions of the Middle Ages. But with prophecy we are dealing with time, itself as mysterious as space, and as difficult to describe since time, like space, is without limits.

For although time has been measured down to microseconds, there may be a question as to which way it flows—not only forward as we conceive it but (as some astronomers have suggested) in a curve or a circle and even backward. The very latest knowledge we have amassed concerning time and space leaves us with much information, but still in a conceptual vacuum, within which the predictions and forecasts from what we term the "dark ages" seem to regain a possible validity—one which they have never really lost.

The end of the world in our lifetime has been dramatically predicted by a number of prophets, many of whom lived in the far past and were unaware of our present B.C. and A.D. system of counting years. These ancient prophecies were, instead, tied to the passage of other events which, when translated to our own system of counting years, come together across time and cultures in indicating that the end of the world as we know it will take place in our calendar system within a few years of A.D. 2000. Before 1945 it was considerably less conceivable that humanity could suddenly perish, especially at a time period so uncomfortably close at hand. But at the present time, with 50,000 warheads poised for launching among contending powers and more in the process of manufacture, the sudden end of mankind does not seem so implausible.

Those who made the ancient prophecies concerning a final catastrophe in the far future were naturally unaware that their warnings of disaster coincided with other predictions made in different parts of the world, areas where religious tradition and belief were especially pronounced—the Middle East, Southern Asia, Northern Africa, prehistoric America, and medieval Europe. It is noteworthy that the dates given for a future day of doom or Judgment Day, when we compare our own system of counting with the equivalent time in other more ancient systems, coincide to a remarkable degree. In addition, several prophecies made within the last 500 years should be considered since these prophecies were made well in advance along with other predictions which later came true.

In the dim ages of pre-history India had established a system of counting years that is still paramount in the astronomic and religious calculations of the Hindus. The present cycle is called the Kali Yuga (the age of Kali, one of whose manifestations is the Goddess of Death) and this will come to an end, as well as the present world, at the beginning of the twenty-first century— A.D. 2000.

According to the Old Testament, notably in Daniel (11, 12), Ezekiel (36, 37, 38), Joel (2, 3), and Isaiah (23, 24), and references in St. Luke and in St. Matthew, the Day of Judgment will come *after* the return of the Jews to Israel and a final battle when the Lord will have gathered "all nations against Jerusalem to battle." At this time there will be "wonders in the heavens and in the earth, blood, and fire, and pillars of smoke . . ." and "many that sleep in the dust of Earth shall awake, some to everlasting life and some to shame and contempt."

Hal Lindsey *(The Late Great Planet Earth)* has found in the Old Testament and Revelation prophetic verses which seem to detail a future battle plan with the attackers of Israel clearly indicated from the direction of their assaults although not by their nationality or political groupings, whose names did not exist in ancient times, but which now are familiar to everyone.

Of special significance is a prophecy of the Final Judgment from Christ Himself as reported by St. Luke and St. Matthew: ". . . Nation shall rise against nation, and kingdom against kingdom . . . and when ye shall see Jerusalem compassed with armies, then know that the desolation thereof is nigh . . . And there shall be signs in the sun, and in the moon, and in the stars; and upon the earth distress of nations, . . . the sea and the waves roaring . . . when ye see these things come to pass, know ye that the kingdom of God is nigh at hand. . . ."

Among the Buddhists there exists a tradition that the world will end 2500 years after the birth of Gautama Buddha which, as he was reputedly born in 500 B.C., would make the end of the present world come at about A.D. 2000. Tibetan Buddhist tradition has long held that the world would end a few years after the Dalai Lama

left Tibet. He left Tibet, pursued by the Chinese Red
Army, in 1951. Another Buddhist tradition from the
high ranges of Central Asia, a prophecy popularly believed to have emanated from the legendary King of the
World, living in the subterranean city of Arghati, fore-
tells that the end of the world will come shortly after the
beginning of the Third World War. This prophecy was
made hundreds of years before many of the details of
the two World Wars that we know could have been
imagined; nevertheless they were detailed in the Arghati prophecy.

Moslem tradition does not specify the date of the
world's ending but tells that it will come soon after men
have walked on the moon. (Some Moslem commentators, however, have suggested that astronauts have
not yet walked on the real moon, but on another false
one, a theory independently depicted in a popular US
film made several years ago.)

The Shiite Moslems, who trace their religious descent from Mohammed's nephew and who form the majority of the Moslem population in Iran and Pakistan,
expect a basic change in the world and the Day of Judgment with the appearance of the twelfth Imam, who
may already be living in this century and whose identity
will soon be revealed.

The Aztecs and associated Amerindian peoples
predicted the end will come at the end of the fourth
"world" or age cycle, called "the World of Fire," due
within the next few years. The Hopi of Arizona believe
that a fatal dark planet, even now hurtling toward the
earth but still invisible, will be announced by a strange
blue flower blooming in the desert. (The flower has already been found.)

An unusual medieval prophecy indicates that the

end of the world will come with the death of the last pope. This prophecy was contained in a list of future popes, compiled by St. Malachy, the Archbishop of Armagh, Ireland, in the twelfth century. The list gives descriptions of the origins, distinguishing features, and reigns of all popes up to the last, when Rome will be destroyed and Judgment Day will come. The last pope will be called Peter and, according to St. Malachy's prophecy, he will be the pope following the pope now reigning.

Nostradamus, the most renowned prophet of the late Middle Ages, was a sixteenth-century French scholar with an uncanny ability of foretelling events which would occur not only during his lifetime but also hundreds of years after his death. He successfully foretold the beginning and the end of the British Empire (before it started), the French Revolution and the execution of the monarchs, World Wars I and II, their results, and the aircraft and bombing of cities from the air, as well as the careers of Napoleon and Hitler, and even allusions through nationality and actions to Khomeni and Khadaffi. His prophecies were expressed in poetic quatrains, generally easy to understand but seldom giving an exact date. But in regard to a world catastrophe his style shifted from apparent riddles to a clear warning when he established that it would occur during the seventh month of 1999.

An American prophet, Edgar Cayce, who made his prophecies upon being questioned while in a semisleeping state, is notable because of the accuracy of his prophecies made years in advance of the event. These predictions describe in some detail events that had not yet happened, such as the deaths of two presidents recently in office, the assassination of one of them, and the assassination of a potential president, civil commotion, seismic upheavals, the development of laser and maser, unknown at the time he described them as simply crystal power—which they are. His description of what would happen after his death in 1945 seems to be fulfilling itself. His predictions went to the year 2001—but no further.

As if the implicit menace of the atomic age were not enough, mankind is now facing a series of other dangers, generally the product of unrestrained industrial exploitation of the resources of the earth. This has become especially noticeable since the burgeoning population of the earth has tripled itself in the last fifty years to a point which, even with more efficient means of distribution, there will simply not be enough food for the earth's peoples.

The seas and oceans are being poisoned by chemical products, oil, industrial and human waste. On land, especially in the industrial countries where most waste is "manufactured," there is increasingly little room to bury it and even when buried, noxious elements leech out and imperil the health of the area. An even greater problem is the disposal of atomic waste, unsafe to dump into the sea and even more unsafe to bury under the land. An alternate possibility—that of sending it out to space—would perhaps entail other dangers not immediately apparent.

The progressive destruction of the earth's rain forests by cutting (an estimated fourteen acres every minute) is constantly decreasing the production of oxygen (and rainfall) necessary for life, while other forests in Europe and North America are being poisoned by acid rain. The present greenhouse effect of overheating the earth by excessive fuels in the atmosphere may cause

183

the melting of the polar glaciers with resultant raising of the level of the oceans and the production of another Great Flood.

The first indication that the development of atomic power during peacetime represented a danger to the surrounding community occurred at a Soviet plutonium plant at Kyshtym in the winter of 1957–1958. This happened when the plutonium fallout from insufficiently stored waste caused a blast which killed hundreds—perhaps thousands—of people. As a result of the wasteland that occurred with the evacuation of people from the immediate and surrounding territory, more than thirty towns were deleted from Soviet maps and a declaration of off limits of the affected area continued until the contaminated soil could be covered with new soil and sand by groups of condemned prisoners, many of whom later died from radiation. More extensive publicity was given the incident at Three Mile Island in 1979 and the Chernobyl meltdown of April and May 1986 with the production of what threatened to be delayed death clouds over Central and Southern Europe, showing the danger of atomic meltdown with its resultant poisoning of the air, water, land, people, animals, and food to be as potentially dangerous to the world and its inhabitants as atomic warfare.

With increasing frequency we are informed through the media of industrial accidents some of which, like the chemical-insecticide disaster in Bhopal, India, killing thousands of persons while they slept, rested, ate, or ran, resemble the sudden plagues of the Middle Ages. Another disaster, caused by cumulative chemical poisoning, took place at the Love Canal, New York State, USA, where a toxic chemical dump was insufficiently buried and was found to have been responsible for serious birth defects in infants which, in the event that the infants survived, could be transmitted and presage the poisoning, as with atomic fallout, of future generations. In Minamata, Japan, villagers developed brain and nerve damage and died as a result of eating fish already poisoned by methyl mercury, dumped into the sea from a nearby factory.

The animal food chain has been broken by the extinction of animal species by man. With the development of improved industrial fishing techniques, sections of the seas and oceans are being fished out at an increasing tempo. Large parts of the world, such as the Sahel Belt across mid-Africa, are in a state of acute starvation with little possibility of cure except permanent aid given by other countries. This same situation, the exhaustion of the soil and killing off of the herds, is being repeated in various parts of the Third World and represents an almost insoluble problem within the limits of present international cooperation. Hunger in the Third World has increased the tempo of the slaughter of most of the world's remaining wild animals, whose population has decreased by 90 percent of what it was fifty years ago.

But despite the alarming tendencies of over-population and overindustrialization that affect our planet, the menace of thermonuclear warfare remains paramount. Those of us who were adults before 1945 possess an outlook on the world that those born after 1945 cannot have. Life before 1945 could certainly be dangerous but never helpless, never threatening of a sudden and complete doom of the whole world as does the outbreak of a nuclear war with its estimated initial casualties of one or two billion people and presumable poisoning of most of the survivors.

Perhaps the most definite prophecy comes from

the Ararat Ark, constituting as it does a memory of a warning. The story is common to Judaism, Christianity, and Islam, the "three religions of the Book," but it was in early Christianity that the Ark became paramount as a religious symbol. In the era of pagan Rome, when official disapproval of Christians often resulted in death in the arena or torture in the imperial prisons, rough sketches of a fish or an ark predated the cross as a sign of recognition in the catacombs or elsewhere. While the fish was used to employ in Greek letters the initials of Jesus, Son of God, Redeemer, the Ark symbol represented the judgment of God and hope for salvation.

Although the Ark story belongs to the Old Testament, frequent references to it as an article of faith occur in Matthew 24, 1 Peter 3 and 2 Peter 2, Romans 1, and Hebrews 2. Certain references in St. Matthew and St. Luke have been interpreted by some researchers to mean that the finding of the Ark will herald the return of the Son of Man and the Last Judgment, especially Luke 17: "And as it was in the days of Noe, so shall it be also in the days of the Son of man." And 17:27: "They did eat, they drank, they married wives, they were given in marriage, until the day that Noe entered into the Ark, and the flood came, and destroyed them all."

As we approach the second millennium an increasing number of people doubt that we will survive into the next one. This point of view is logically based on the apparent inability or unwillingness of mankind to take the necessary steps to avoid the destructive processes that he himself has unleashed: nuclear warfare that will affect victor, vanquished, and neutrals alike; pillage and destruction of the earth's resources; and pollution and chemical poisoning of earth's lands, oceans, and skies. We are reminded of Genesis 6: "And God saw that the wickedness of man was great in the earth, and that every imagination of the thoughts of his heart was only evil continually."

Noah was warned and through his actions others could take heed, which they did not. But this time man has warned himself through the various nuclear and chemical accidents that are taking place at an increasing tempo. The Biblical promise of the rainbow has not been broken: this time man seems to have decided by himself to take the road of self-destruction.

The Ararat Ark is a reminder of man's possible fate but this time it is not the vehicle of salvation. For there is another Ark which may serve. All we have to do when we find it is to repair it and make it safe for a long journey. It is far from legendary but in a place so obvious that no one has realized where it is. It is already provisioned with food and water, is as yet uncontaminated, and there is space for a crew much larger than that which boarded the Ark or the other survival ships of legend. The animals, those that have survived, are already on board. The Ark is built to weather great storms, as tumultuous as any encountered by the Ark of Noah. There will be no need to send forth a dove to find out if the Flood has abated since the catastrophes that this other Ark must surmount are of a different kind from the Flood of Noah. The Ark too is different. It is essentially a vessel but it navigates in an ocean vast beyond measure.

For this time, the Ark is the earth itself.

Acknowledgments

Grateful acknowledgment is made to the following persons for their contributions to this book through their information, research, photographs, drawings, maps, or reports on mountain-climbing expeditions. It should be expressly understood that these persons do not necessarily share the author's theories or opinions expressed in *The Lost Ship of Noah.*

Ahmet Ali Arslan, artist, photographer, writer, alpinist, editor, radio producer, PhD Atatürk University
Valerie Seary Berlitz, author, editor, artist, photographer, researcher

Lin Berlitz, researcher
Jay Bitzer, Probe Ministries photographer, alpinist
Ben Bothrop, Lieutenant Colonel, USAF ret.
Patricia Campbell-Horton, author, historian
Gloria Cashin, mathematician, geologist
Bill Crouse, writer, editor: Probe Ministries, alpinist, expedition leader on Ararat
Eryl Cummings, alpinist, frequent expedition leader on Ararat
Violet Cummings, author
Sheik M. S. Dien, teacher: Islamic Law, Al Ahzar University, Cairo (through the courtesy of Dorothy Ashford, researcher in history and religion)
David Fasold, Captain USMS, diver, salvor, underwater explorer, writer, archaeological researcher
Carlos González G., theologian, Bible scholar

James T. Hashian, author; public affairs officer, US government

George Hauser, photographer

Lloyd Hawkins, Lieutenant Colonel, USAF ret.

Edward Kuhnel, international lawyer, lecturer

Elfred Lee, artist, alpinist, writer

Ivan Lee, archaeologist, artist, editor, publisher, writer

John McIntosh, educator, researcher, alpinist

René Noorbergen, author, photographer, foreign correspondent

Antonio Pascual F., author, historian, educator

J. L. Pennington, Colonel, USAF ret.

Kenneth Peters, historian, Lieutenant Colonel, USA ret.

Robert Phillips, Colonel, USAF ret.

The late Alexei Nikolaevich Romanov, reputed son of the last Russian Tsar

Herbert Sawinski, archaeologist, explorer, diver, pilot, writer, director of the Fort Lauderdale Museum of Archaeology

Zecharia Sitchin, author, linguist specializing in ancient languages of the Middle East, archaeologist, researcher, Bible scholar, philosopher

The late Egerton Sykes, author, linguist, editor, publisher, explorer, British Foreign Service Officer, with especial appreciation of his contribution to the author of his contemporary and historical Ark file

Bradley Tellshaw, Colonel, USAF ret.

J. Manson Valentine, naturalist, paleontologist, archaeologist, explorer, diver, author, Curator Honoris, Museum of Science, Miami; Research Associate of the Bishop Museum, Honolulu

Bob Warth, researcher, writer, editor, president of the Society for the Investigation of the Unexplained

Phyllis Watson, researcher, writer

Walter Wood, engineer, explorer

And with special appreciation to Phyllis Grann, publisher, and Audrey Cusson, editor, for their encouragement and advice in the publication of *The Lost Ship of Noah*.

Bibliography

Bailey, Lloyd R. *Where Is Noah's Ark?*: Nashville, 1978.
Balsiger, Dave, and Sellier, Charles E., Jr. *In Search of Noah's Ark*: Los Angeles, 1976.
Berlitz, Charles. *Atlantis: The Eighth Continent*: New York, 1984.
——. *The Bermuda Triangle*: New York, 1974.
——. *Doomsday 1999 A.D.*: New York, 1981.
Campbell, Roger F. *A Place to Hide*: Wheaton, 1983.
Ceram, C. W. *Götter, Gräber and Gelehrte*: Hamburg, 1949.
Cummings, Violet. *Has Anybody Really Seen Noah's Ark?*: San Diego, 1983.
——. *Noah's Ark: Fact or Fable?*: San Diego, 1972.
Von Däniken, Erich, *Chariots of the Gods?*: New York, 1977.
Garrison, Webb, *Strange Facts About the Bible*: New York, 1976.
Hapgood, Charles. *Earth's Shifting Crust*: Philadelphia, 1958.
——. *Maps of the Ancient Sea Kings*: New York, 1966.
——. *The Path of the Pole*: New York, 1970.
Irwin, James B. *More Than an Ark on Ararat*: Nashville, 1978.
LaHaye, Tim, and Morris, John. *The Ark on Ararat*: Nashville, 1976.
LeVert, Liberté, *The Prophecies and Enigmas of Nostradamus*: New Jersey, 1979.
Lindsey, Hal. *The Late Great Planet Earth*: New York, 1970.
Marston, Charles. *La Bible a dit vrai*: Paris, 1952.
Montgomery, John Warwick. *The Quest for Noah's Ark*: Winona Lake, 1977.
Morris, Henry M. *The Bible and Modern Science*: Chicago, 1951.
Morris, John D. *Adventure on Ararat*: San Diego, 1973.
Navarra, Fernand. *The Forbidden Mountain*: London, 1956.
——. *J'ai trouvé l'arche de Noé*: Paris, 1956.
Noorbergen, René B. *The Ark File*: Mountain View, CA, 1972.
Ossendowski, Ferdinand. *Bestias, Hombres, Dioses*: Madrid, 1964.
Parrot, André. *Déluge et arche de Noé*: Paris, 1952.

Parrot, J. J. Friedrich. *Journey to Ararat*: London, 1845.
Platt, Rutherford H., Jr., ed. *The Forgotten Books of Eden*: New York, 1981.
Shirer, William T. *Twentieth Century Journey*: New York, 1976.
Sitchin, Zecharia. *The Stairway to Heaven*: New York, 1980.
——. *The Twelfth Planet*: New York, 1976.
Summers, Anthony, and Mengold, Tom. *The File on the Tsar*: London, 1976.
Teeple, Howard M. *The Noah's Ark Nonsense*: Evanston, 1978.
Velikovsky, Immanuel. *Earth in Upheaval*: Garden City, 1955.
——. *Worlds in Collision*: Garden City, 1955.
Waters, Frank, and White Bear. *Book of the Hopi*: New York, 1969.
Wilkins, Harold T. *Secret Cities of Old South America*: London, 1952.
Zanot, Mario. *Dopo il Diluvio*: Milan, 1974.

And the following works from medieval or ancient times:

The Bible, King James Version
The Koran, translated by E. H. Palmer: London, 1947.
The Mahabharata, translated by Protap Chandra Roy: Calcutta, 1889.
Berossus: *History of Babylonia.*
Epiphanius of Salamis: *Panarion of Heresies.*
Josephus: *Antiquities of the Jews.*
Marco Polo: *Travels.*
Nicolaus of Damascus: *Universal History.*
Olearius (Oelschläger), *Voyages curieux.*
and selected writings of

    Sir John Chardin.
    Sir John Mandeville.
    Odoric.
    John Chrysostom.

Index

Index

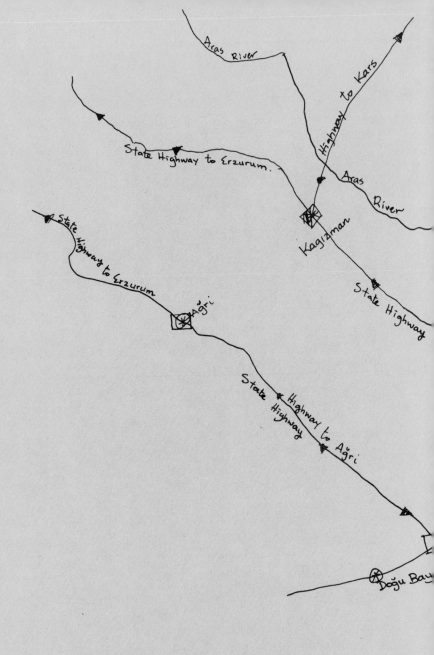

Great Ararat and Little Ararat are located within several miles of the USSR to the northeast and Iran to the southeast. The principal Turkish roads leading to and from the mountain to the town of Doğubayazit, the jumping-off place for the exploration of Ararat, are shown. On the lower left the village of Uzengili (formerly Mahşer) is indicated, close to the site of the shiplike mound under which a large craft may be buried—the ancient ship of Noah. Map © 1986 by Ahmet Ali Arslan